W9-BJZ-774

MAXnotes®

William Shakespeare's

Antony and Cleopatra

Text by
John Foss
(M.A., Duke University)
Department of English
University of South Carolina at Beaufort
Beaufort, South Carolina

Illustrations by
Georges LaVigne

Research & Education Association

MAXnotes® for
ANTONY AND CLEOPATRA

Printed in the United States of America

Library of Congress Catalog Card Number 96-67443

International Standard Book Number 0-87891-002-6

MAXnotes® is a registered trademark of
Research & Education Association, Piscataway, New Jersey 08854

What **MAXnotes®** Will Do for You

This book is intended to help you absorb the essential contents and features of William Shakespeare's *Antony and Cleopatra* and to help you gain a thorough understanding of the work. The book has been designed to do this more quickly and effectively than any other study guide.

For best results, this **MAXnotes** book should be used as a companion to the actual work, not instead of it. The interaction between the two will greatly benefit you.

To help you in your studies, this book presents the most up-to-date interpretations of every section of the actual work, followed by questions and fully explained answers that will enable you to analyze the material critically. The questions also will help you to test your understanding of the work and will prepare you for discussions and exams.

Meaningful illustrations are included to further enhance your understanding and enjoyment of the literary work. The illustrations are designed to place you into the mood and spirit of the work's settings.

The **MAXnotes** also include summaries, character lists, explanations of plot, and scene by scene analyses. A biography of the author and discussion of the work's historical context will help you put this literary piece into the proper perspective of what is taking place.

The use of this study guide will save you the hours of preparation time that would ordinarily be required to arrive at a complete grasp of this work of literature. You will be well prepared for classroom discussions, homework, and exams. The guidelines that are included for writing papers and reports on various topics will prepare you for any added work which may be assigned.

The **MAXnotes** will take your grades "to the max."

Dr. Max Fogiel
Program Director

Contents

**Each Scene includes List of Characters,
Summary, Analysis, Study Questions and
Answers, and Suggested Essay Topics.**

SECTION ONE

Introduction

The Life and Work of William Shakespeare

The details of William Shakespeare's life are sketchy, mostly mere surmise based upon court or other clerical records. His parents, John and Mary (Arden), were married about 1557; she was of the landed gentry, and he was a yeoman—a glover and commodities merchant. By 1568, John had risen through the ranks of town government and held the position of high bailiff, which was a position similar to mayor. William, the eldest son and the third of eight children, was born in 1564, probably on April 23, several days before his baptism on April 26 in Stratford-upon-Avon. Shakespeare is also believed to have died on the same date—April 23—in 1616.

It is believed that William attended the local grammar school in Stratford where his parents lived, and that he studied primarily Latin, rhetoric, logic, and literature. Shakespeare probably left school at age 15, which was the norm, to take a job, especially since this was the period of his father's financial difficulty. At age 18 (1582), William married Anne Hathaway, a local farmer's daughter who was eight years his senior. Their first daughter (Susanna) was born six months later (1583), and twins, Judith and Hamnet, were born in 1585.

Shakespeare's life can be divided into three periods: the first 20 years in Stratford, which include his schooling, early marriage, and fatherhood; the next 25 years as an actor and playwright in London; and the last five in retirement in Stratford where he enjoyed moderate wealth gained from his theatrical successes. The years linking the first two periods are marked by a lack of information about Shakespeare, and are often referred to as the "dark years."

At some point during the "dark years," Shakespeare began his career with a London theatrical company, perhaps in 1589, for he was already an actor and playwright of some note by 1592. Shakespeare apparently wrote and acted for numerous theatrical companies, including Pembroke's Men, and Strange's Men, which later became the Chamberlain's Men, with whom he remained for the rest of his career.

In 1592, the Plague closed the theaters for about two years, and Shakespeare turned to writing book-length narrative poetry. Most notable were *Venus and Adonis* and *The Rape of Lucrece*, both of which were dedicated to the Earl of Southampton, whom scholars accept as Shakespeare's friend and benefactor despite a lack of documentation. During this same period, Shakespeare was writing his sonnets, which are more likely signs of the time's fashion rather than actual love poems detailing any particular relationship. He returned to playwriting when theaters reopened in 1594, and did not continue to write poetry. His sonnets were published without his consent in 1609, shortly before his retirement.

Amid all of his success, Shakespeare suffered the loss of his only son, Hamnet, who died in 1596 at the age of 11. But Shakespeare's career continued unabated, and in London in 1599, he became one of the partners in the new Globe Theater, which was built by the Chamberlain's Men.

Shakespeare wrote very little after 1612, which was the year he completed *Henry VIII*. It was during a performance of this play in 1613 that the Globe caught fire and burned to the ground. Sometime between 1610 and 1613, Shakespeare returned to Stratford, where he owned a large house and property, to spend his remaining years with his family.

William Shakespeare died on April 23, 1616, and was buried two days later in the chancel of Holy Trinity Church, where he had been baptized exactly 52 years earlier. His literary legacy included 37 plays, 154 sonnets, and five major poems.

Incredibly, most of Shakespeare's plays had never been published in anything except pamphlet form, and were simply extant as acting scripts stored at the Globe. Theater scripts were not regarded as literary works of art, but only the basis for the performance. Plays were simply a popular form of entertainment for all layers of society in Shakespeare's time. Only the efforts of two of Shakespeare's company, John Heminges and Henry Condell, preserved his 36 plays (minus *Pericles*, the thirty-seventh).

Shakespeare's Language

Shakespeare's language can create a strong pang of intimidation, even fear, in a large number of modern-day readers. Fortunately, however, this need not be the case. All that is needed to master the art of reading Shakespeare is to practice the techniques of unraveling uncommonly-structured sentences and to become familiar with the poetic use of uncommon words. We must realize that during the 400-year span between Shakespeare's time and our own, both the way we live and speak has changed. Although most of his vocabulary is in use today, some of it is obsolete, and what may be most confusing is that some of his words are used today, but with slightly different or totally different meanings. On the stage, actors readily dissolve these language stumbling blocks. They study Shakespeare's dialogue and express it dramatically in word and in action so that its meaning is graphically enacted. If the reader studies Shakespeare's lines as an actor does, looking up and reflecting upon the meaning of unfamiliar words until real voice is discovered, he or she will suddenly experience the excitement, the depth and the sheer poetry of what these characters say.

Shakespeare's Sentences

In English, or any other language, the meaning of a sentence greatly depends upon where each word is placed in that sentence. "The child hurt the mother" and "The mother hurt the child" have opposite meanings, even though the words are the same, simply because the words are arranged differently. Because word position is so integral to English, the reader will find unfamiliar word arrangements confusing, even difficult to understand. Since Shakespeare's plays are poetic dramas, he often shifts from average word arrangements to the strikingly unusual so that the line will conform to the desired poetic rhythm. Often, too, Shakespeare employs unusual word order to afford a character his own specific style of speaking.

Today, English sentence structure follows a sequence of subject first, verb second, and an optional object third. Shakespeare, however, often places the verb before the subject, which reads, "Speaks he" rather than "He speaks." Solanio speaks with this inverted structure in *The Merchant of Venice* stating, "I should be still/ Plucking the grass to know where sits the wind" (Bevington edition, I, i, ll.17-19), while today's standard English word order would have the clause at the end of this line read, "where the wind sits." "Wind" is the subject of this clause, and "sits" is the verb. Bassanio's words in Act Two also exemplify this inversion: "And in such eyes as ours appear not faults" (II, ii, l. 184). In our normal word order, we would say, "Faults do not appear in eyes such as ours," with "faults" as the subject in both Shakespeare's word order and ours.

Inversions like these are not troublesome, but when Shakespeare positions the predicate adjective or the object before the subject and verb, we are sometimes surprised. For example, rather than "I saw him," Shakespeare may use a structure such as "Him I saw." Similarly, "Cold the morning is" would be used for our "The morning is cold." Lady Macbeth demonstrates this inversion as she speaks of her husband: "Glamis thou art, and Cawdor, and shalt be/What thou art promised" (Macbeth, I, v, ll. 14-15). In current English word order, this quote would begin, "Thou art Glamis, and Cawdor."

In addition to inversions, Shakespeare purposefully keeps words apart that we generally keep together. To illustrate, consider Bassanio's humble admission in *The Merchant of Venice*: "I owe you much, and, like a wilful youth,/That which I owe is lost" (I, i, ll. 146-147). The phrase, "like a wilful youth," separates the regular sequence of "I owe you much" and "That which I owe is lost." To understand more clearly this type of passage, the reader could rearrange these word groups into our conventional order: I owe you much and I wasted what you gave me because I was young and impulsive. While these rearranged clauses will sound like normal English, and will be simpler to understand, they will no longer have the desired poetic rhythm, and the emphasis will now be on the wrong words.

As we read Shakespeare, we will find words that are separated by long, interruptive statements. Often subjects are separated from verbs, and verbs are separated from objects. These long interruptions can be used to give a character dimension or to add an element of suspense. For example, in *Romeo and Juliet* Benvolio describes both Romeo's moodiness and his own sensitive and thoughtful nature:

> I, measuring his affections by my own,
> Which then most sought, where most might not be found,
> Being one too many by my weary self,
> Pursu'd my humour, not pursuing his,
> And gladly shunn'd who gladly fled from me.
> (I, i, ll. 126-130)

In this passage, the subject "I" is distanced from its verb "Pursu'd." The long interruption serves to provide information which is integral to the plot. Another example, taken from *Hamlet*, is the ghost, Hamlet's father, who describes Hamlet's uncle, Claudius, as

> ...that incestuous, that adulterate beast,
> With witchcraft of his wit, with traitorous gifts—
> O wicked wit and gifts, that have the power
> So to seduce—won to his shameful lust
> The will of my most seeming virtuous queen.
> (I, v, ll. 43-47)

From this we learn that Prince Hamlet's mother is the victim of an evil seduction and deception. The delay between the subject, "beast," and the verb, "won," creates a moment of tension filled with the image of a cunning predator waiting for the right moment to spring into attack. This interruptive passage allows the play to unfold crucial information and thus to build the tension necessary to produce a riveting drama.

While at times these long delays are merely for decorative purposes, they are often used to narrate a particular situation or to enhance character development. As *Antony and Cleopatra* opens, an interruptive passage occurs in the first few lines. Although the delay is not lengthy, Philo's words vividly portray Antony's military prowess while they also reveal the immediate concern of the drama. Antony is distracted from his career, and is now focused on Cleopatra:

> ...those goodly eyes,
> That o'er the files and musters of the war
> Have glow'd like plated Mars, now bend, now turn
> The office and devotion of their view
> Upon a tawny front.... (I, i, ll. 2-6)

Whereas Shakespeare sometimes heaps detail upon detail, his sentences are often elliptical, that is, they omit words we expect in written English sentences. In fact, we often do this in our spoken conversations. For instance, we say, "You see that?" when we really mean, "Did you see that?" Reading poetry or listening to lyrics in music conditions us to supply the omitted words and it makes us more comfortable reading this type of dialogue. Consider one passage in *The Merchant of Venice* where Antonio's friends ask him why he seems so sad and Solanio tells Antonio, "Why, then you are in love" (I, i, l. 46). When Antonio denies this, Solanio responds, "Not in love neither?" (I, i, l. 47). The word "you" is omitted but understood despite the confusing double negative.

In addition to leaving out words, Shakespeare often uses intentionally vague language, a strategy which taxes the reader's attentiveness. In *Antony and Cleopatra*, Cleopatra, upset that Antony is leaving for Rome after learning that his wife died in battle, convinces him to stay in Egypt:

> Sir, you and I must part, but that's not it:
> Sir you and I have lov'd, but there's not it;
> That you know well, something it is I would—
> O, my oblivion is a very Antony,
> And I am all forgotten.
> (I, iii, ll. 87-91, emphasis added)

In line 89, "...something it is I would" suggests that there is something that she would want to say, do, or have done. The intentional vagueness leaves us, and certainly Antony, to wonder. Though this sort of writing may appear lackadaisical for all that it leaves out, here the vagueness functions to portray Cleopatra as rhetorically sophisticated. Similarly, when asked what thing a crocodile is (meaning Antony himself who is being compared to a crocodile), Antony slyly evades the question by giving a vague reply:

> It is shap'd, sir, like itself, and it is as broad as it hath
> breadth. It is just so high as it is, and moves with it own
> organs. It lives by that which nourisheth it, and, the
> elements once out of it, it transmigrates.
> (II, vii, ll. 43-46)

This kind of evasiveness, or doubletalk, occurs often in Shakespeare's writing and requires extra patience on the part of the reader.

Shakespeare's Words

As we read Shakespeare's plays, we will encounter uncommon words. Many of these words are not in use today. As *Romeo and Juliet* opens, we notice words like "shrift" (confession) and "holidame" (a holy relic). Words like these should be explained in notes to the text. Shakespeare also employs words which we still use, though with different meaning. For example, in *The Merchant of Venice* "caskets" refer to small, decorative chests for holding jewels. However, modern readers may think of a large cask instead of the smaller, diminutive casket.

Another trouble modern readers will have with Shakespeare's English is with words that are still in use today, but which mean something different in Elizabethan use. In *The Merchant of Venice*, Shakespeare uses the word "straight" (as in "straight away") where we would say "immediately." Here, the modern reader is unlikely to carry away the wrong message, however, since the modern meaning will simply make no sense. In this case, textual notes will clarify a phrase's meaning. To cite another example, in *Romeo and Juliet*, after Mercutio dies, Romeo states that the "black fate on moe days doth depend" (emphasis added). In this case, "depend" really means "impend."

Shakespeare's Wordplay

All of Shakespeare's works exhibit his mastery of playing with language and with such variety that many people have authored entire books on this subject alone. Shakespeare's most frequently used types of wordplay are common: metaphors, similes, synecdoche and metonymy, personification, allusion, and puns. It is when Shakespeare violates the normal use of these devices, or rhetorical figures, that the language becomes confusing.

A metaphor is a comparison in which an object or idea is replaced by another object or idea with common attributes. For example, in *Macbeth* a murderer tells Macbeth that Banquo has been murdered, as directed, but that his son, Fleance, escaped, having witnessed his father's murder. Fleance, now a threat to Macbeth, is described as a serpent:

> There the grown serpent lies, the worm that's fled
> Hath nature that in time will venom breed,
> No teeth for the present. (III, iv, ll. 29-31, emphasis added)

Similes, on the other hand, compare objects or ideas while using the words "like" or "as." In *Romeo and Juliet,* Romeo tells Juliet that "Love goes toward love as schoolboys from their books" (II, ii, l. 156). Such similes often give way to more involved comparisons, "extended similes." For example, Juliet tells Romeo:

> 'Tis almost morning, I would have thee gone,
> And yet no farther than a wonton's bird,
> That lets it hop a little from his hand
> Like a poor prisoner in his twisted gyves,
> And with silken thread plucks it back again,
> So loving-jealous of his liberty.
> (II, ii, ll. 176-181, emphasis added)

An epic simile, a device borrowed from heroic poetry, is an extended simile that builds into an even more elaborate comparison. In *Macbeth*, Macbeth describes King Duncan's virtues with an angelic, celestial simile and then drives immediately into another simile that redirects us into a vision of warfare and destruction:

> ...Besides this Duncan
> Hath borne his faculties so meek, hath been
> So clear in his great office, that his virtues
> Will plead like angels, trumpet-tongued, against
> The deep damnation of his taking-off;
> And pity, like a naked new-born babe,
> Striding the blast, or heaven's cherubim, horsed
> Upon the sightless couriers of the air,
> Shall blow the horrid deed in every eye,
> That tears shall drown the wind....
> (I, vii, ll. 16-25, emphasis added)

Shakespeare employs other devices, like synecdoche and metonymy, to achieve "verbal economy," or using one or two words to express more than one thought. Synecdoche is a figure of speech using a part for the whole. An example of synecdoche is using the word boards to imply a stage. Boards are only a small part of the materials that make up a stage, however, the term boards has become a colloquial synonym for stage. Metonymy is a figure of speech using the name of one thing for that of another which it is associated. An example of metonymy is using crown to mean the king (as used in the sentence "These lands belong to the crown"). Since a crown is associated with or an attribute of the king, the word crown has become a metonymy for the king. It is important to understand that every metonymy is a synecdoche, but not every synecdoche is a metonymy. This is rule is true because a metonymy must not only be a part of the root word, making a synecdoche, but also be a unique attribute of or associated with the root word.

Synecdoche and metonymy in Shakespeare's works is often very confusing to a new student because he creates uses for words that they usually do not perform. This technique is often complicated and yet very subtle, which makes it difficult of a new student to dissect and understand. An example of these devices in one of Shakespeare's plays can be found in *The Merchant of Venice* . In warning his daughter, Jessica, to ignore the Christian revelries in the streets below, Shylock says:

Lock up my doors; and when you hear the drum
And the vile squealing of the wry-necked fife,
Clamber not you up to the casements then...
(I, v, ll. 30-32)

The phrase of importance in this quote is "the wry-necked fife."
When a reader examines this phrase it does not seem to make
sense; a fife is a cylinder-shaped instrument, there is no part of it
that can be called a neck. The phrase then must be taken to refer
to the fife-player, who has to twist his or her neck to play the fife.
Fife, therefore, is a synecdoche for fife-player, much as boards is
for stage. The trouble with understanding this phrase is that "vile
squealing" logically refers to the sound of the fife, not the fife-
player, and the reader might be led to take fife as the instrument
because of the parallel reference to "drum" in the previous line.
The best solution to this quandary is that Shakespeare uses the
word fife to refer to both the instrument and the player. Both the
player and the instrument are needed to complete the wordplay
in this phrase, which, though difficult to understand to new readers, cannot be seen as a flaw since Shakespeare manages to
convey two meanings with one word. This remarkable example
of synecdoche illuminates Shakespeare's mastery of "verbal
economy."

Shakespeare also uses vivid and imagistic wordplay through
personification, in which human capacities and behaviors are at-
tributed to inanimate objects. Bassanio, in *The Merchant of Venice*,
almost speechless when Portia promises to marry him and share
all her worldly wealth, states "my blood speaks to you in my veins..."
(III, ii, l. 176). How deeply he must feel since even his blood can
speak. Similarly, Portia, learning of the penalty that Antonio must
pay for defaulting on his debt, tells Salerio, "There are some shrewd
contents in yond same paper/That steals the color from Bassanio's
cheek" (III, ii, ll. 243-244).

Another important facet of Shakespeare's rhetorical repertoire
is his use of allusion. An allusion is a reference to another author
or to an historical figure or event. Very often Shakespeare alludes
to the heroes and heroines of Ovid's *Metamorphoses*. For example,
in Cymbeline an entire room is decorated with images illustrating

the stories from this classical work, and the heroine, Imogen, has been reading from this text. Similarly, in *Titus Andronicus* characters not only read directly from the *Metamorphoses*, but a subplot re-enacts one of the *Metamorphoses's* most famous stories, the rape and mutilation of Philomel.

Another way Shakespeare uses allusion is to drop names of mythological, historical and literary figures. In *The Taming of the Shrew*, for instance, Petruchio compares Katharina, the woman whom he is courting, to Diana (II, i, l. 55), the virgin goddess, in order to suggest that Katharina is a man-hater. At times, Shakespeare will allude to well-known figures without so much as mentioning their names. In *Twelfth Night*, for example, though the Duke and Valentine are ostensibly interested in Olivia, a rich countess, Shakespeare asks his audience to compare the Duke's emotional turmoil to the plight of Acteon, whom the goddess Diana transforms into a deer to be hunted and killed by Acteon's own dogs:

> Duke: That instant was I turn'd into a hart,
>   And my desires, like fell and cruel hounds,
>   E'er since pursue me.
>   [...]
> Valentine: But like a cloistress she will veiled walk,
>   And water once a day her chamber round....
>   (I, i, l. 20 ff.)

Shakespeare's use of puns spotlights his exceptional wit. His comedies in particular are loaded with puns, usually of a sexual nature. Puns work through the ambiguity that results when multiple senses of a word are evoked; homophones often cause this sort of ambiguity. In *Antony and Cleopatra*, Enobarbus believes "there is mettle in death" (I, ii, l. 146), meaning that there is "courage" in death; at the same time, mettle suggests the homophone metal, referring to swords made of metal causing death. In early editions of Shakespeare's work there was no distinction made between the two words. Antony puns on the word "earing," (I, ii, ll. 112-114) meaning both plowing (as in rooting out weeds) and hearing: he angrily sends away a messenger, not wishing to hear the message from his wife, Fulvia: "...O then we bring forth weeds,/

when our quick minds lie still, and our ills told us/Is as our earing." If ill-natured news is planted in one's "hearing," it will render an "earing" (harvest) of ill-natured thoughts. A particularly clever pun, also in *Antony and Cleopatra,* stands out after Antony's troops have fought Octavius's men in Egypt: "We have beat him to his camp. Run one before,/And let the queen know of our gests" (IV, viii, ll. 1-2). Here "gests" means deeds (in this case, deeds of battle); it is also a pun on "guests," as though Octavius' slain soldiers were to be guests when buried in Egypt.

One should note that Elizabethan pronunciation was in several cases different from our own. Thus, modern readers, especially Americans, will miss out on the many puns based on homophones. The textual notes will point up many of these "lost" puns, however.

Shakespeare's sexual innuendoes can be either clever or tedious depending upon the speaker and situation. The modern reader should recall that sexuality in Shakespeare's time was far more complex than in ours and that characters may refer to such things as masturbation and homosexual activity. Textual notes in some editions will point out these puns but rarely explain them. An example of a sexual pun or innuendo can be found in *The Merchant of Venice* when Portia and Nerissa are discussing Portia's past suitors using innuendo to tell of their sexual prowess:

Portia: I pray thee, overname them, and as thou
            namest them, I will describe them, and
            according to my description level at my
            affection.
Nerrisa: First, there is the Neapolitan prince.
Portia: Ay, that's a colt indeed, for he doth nothing but
            talk of his horse, and he makes it a great
            appropriation to his own good parts that he can
            shoe him himself. I am much afeard my lady his
            mother played false with the smith.
            (I, ii, ll. 35-45)

The "Neapolitan prince" is given a grade of an inexperienced youth when Portia describes him as a "colt." The prince is thought to be inexperienced because he did nothing but "talk of his horse" (a pun for his penis) and his other great attributes. Portia goes on to say that the prince boasted that he could "shoe him [his horse] himself," a possible pun meaning that the prince was very proud that he could masturbate. Finally, Portia makes an attack upon the prince's mother, saying that "my lady his mother played false with the smith," a pun to say his mother must have committed adultery with a blacksmith to give birth to such a vulgar man having an obsession with "shoeing his horse."

It is worth mentioning that Shakespeare gives the reader hints when his characters might be using puns and innuendoes. In *The Merchant of Venice*, Portia's lines are given in prose when she is joking, or engaged in bawdy conversations. Later on the reader will notice that Portia's lines are rhymed in poetry, such as when she is talking in court or to Bassanio. This is Shakespeare's way of letting the reader know when Portia is jesting and when she is serious.

Shakespeare's Dramatic Verse

Finally, the reader will notice that some lines are actually rhymed verse while others are in verse without rhyme; and much of Shakespeare's drama is in prose. Shakespeare usually has his lovers speak in the language of love poetry which uses rhymed couplets. The archetypal example of this comes, of course, from *Romeo and Juliet*:

> The grey-ey'd morn smiles on the frowning night,
> Check'ring the eastern clouds with streaks of light,
> And fleckled darkness like a drunkard reels
> From forth day's path and Titan's fiery wheels.
> (II, iii, ll. 1-4)

Here it is ironic that Friar Lawrence should speak these lines since he is not the one in love. He, therefore, appears buffoonish and out of touch with reality. Shakespeare often has his characters speak in rhymed verse to let the reader know that the character is acting in jest, and vice-versa.

Perhaps the majority of Shakespeare's lines are in blank verse, a form of poetry which does not use rhyme (hence the name blank) but still employs a rhythm native to the English language, iambic pentameter, where every second syllable in a line of ten syllables receives stress. Consider the following verses from *Hamlet*, and note the accents and the lack of end-rhyme:

> The síngle ánd pecúliar lífe is bóund
> With áll the stréngth and ármor óf the mínd
> (III, iii, ll. 12-13)

The final syllable of these verses receives stress and is said to have a hard, or "strong," ending. A soft ending, also said to be "weak," receives no stress. In *The Tempest*, Shakespeare uses a soft ending to shape a verse that demonstrates through both sound (meter) and sense the capacity of the feminine to propagate:

> and thén I lóv'd thee
> And shów'd thee áll the quálitíes o' th' ísle,
> The frésh spríngs, bríne-pits, bárren pláce and fértile.
> (I, ii, ll. 338-40)

The first and third of these lines here have soft endings.

In general, Shakespeare saves blank verse for his characters of noble birth. Therefore, it is significant when his lofty characters speak in prose. Prose holds a special place in Shakespeare's dialogues; he uses it to represent the speech habits of the common people. Not only do lowly servants and common citizens speak in prose, but important, lower class figures also use this fun, at times ribald variety of speech. Though Shakespeare crafts some very ornate lines in verse, his prose can be equally daunting, for some of his characters may speechify and break into doubletalk in their attempts to show sophistication. A clever instance of this comes when the Third Citizen in Coriolanus refers to the people's paradoxical lack of power when they must elect Coriolanus as their new leader once Coriolanus has orated how he has courageously fought for them in battle:

> We have power in ourselves to do it, but it is
> a power that we have no power to do; for if he show us his

wounds and tell us his deeds, we are to put our tongues into those wounds and speak for them; so, if he tell us his noble deeds, we must also tell him our noble acceptance of them. Ingratitude is monstrous, and for the multitude to be ingrateful were to make a monster of the multitude, of the which we, being members, should bring ourselves to be monstrous members.
(II, ii, ll. 3-13)

Notice that this passage contains as many metaphors, hideous though they be, as any other passage in Shakespeare's dramatic verse.

When reading Shakespeare, paying attention to characters who suddenly break into rhymed verse, or who slip into prose after speaking in blank verse, will heighten your awareness of a character's mood and personal development. For instance, in *Antony and Cleopatra*, the famous military leader Marcus Antony usually speaks in blank verse, but also speaks in fits of prose (II, iii, ll. 43-46) once his masculinity and authority have been questioned. Similarly, in *Timon of Athens*, after the wealthy lord Timon abandons the city of Athens to live in a cave, he harangues anyone whom he encounters in prose (IV, iii, l. 331 ff.). In contrast, the reader should wonder why the bestial Caliban in *The Tempest* speaks in blank verse rather than in prose.

Implied Stage Action

When we read a Shakespearean play, we are reading a performance text. Actors interact through dialogue, but at the same time these actors cry, gesticulate, throw tantrums, pick up daggers, and compulsively wash murderous "blood" from their hands. Some of the action that takes place on stage is explicitly stated in stage directions. However, some of the stage activity is couched within the dialogue itself. Attentiveness to these cues is important as one conceives how to visualize the action. When Iago in *Othello* feigns concern for Cassio whom he himself has stabbed, he calls to the surrounding men, "Come, come:/Lend me a light" (V, i, ll. 86-87). It is almost sure that one of the actors involved will bring him a torch or lantern. In the same play, Emilia, Desdemona's maidservant, asks if she should fetch her lady's nightgown and Desdemona replies,

"No, unpin me here" (IV, iii, l. 37). In Macbeth, after killing Duncan, Macbeth brings the murder weapon back with him. When he tells his wife that he cannot return to the scene and place the daggers to suggest that the king's guards murdered Duncan, she castigates him: "Infirm of purpose/Give me the daggers. The sleeping and the dead are but as pictures" (II, ii, ll. 50-52). As she exits, it is easy to visualize Lady Macbeth grabbing the daggers from her husband.

For 400 years, readers have found it greatly satisfying to work with all aspects of Shakespeare's language—the implied stage action, word choice, sentence structure, and wordplay—until all aspects come to life. Just as seeing a fine performance of a Shakespearean play is exciting, staging the play in one's own mind's eye, and revisiting lines to enrich the sense of the action, will enhance one's appreciation of Shakespeare's extraordinary literary and dramatic achievements.

Historical Background

Although Shakespeare was well acquainted with the history and literature of his day and of preceding centuries, he did not hesitate to amend the known facts of history, if it served his dramatic purposes. *Antony and Cleopatra* was not well received when it was first produced. Since then, *Antony and Cleopatra* has grown in favor with both producers and readers. Modern productions have received considerably better reviews, on the whole, than any that were published during the playwright's lifetime.

Antony and Cleopatra is the second in a trilogy of Roman plays (the first was *Julius Caesar;* the third, *Coriolanus*); Shakespeare wrote about an era some 1700 years before his own time. His main source of historical information was Plutarch, whose biographies of great Greeks and Romans has remained a staple of literature for nearly 2,000 years and is still read today.

The famous first triumvirate of Rome—consisting of Julius Caesar, Marcus Crassus, and Pompey the Great—dissolved with the conspiracy of Brutus, Cassius and others against Julius Caesar, and resulted in his assassination. Crassus was murdered by the Parthians, and Pompey the Great was defeated in an uprising against Rome. Following the death of Julius Caesar, the second triumvirate came into being and consisted of Octavius (the adopted son and designated heir of Julius Caesar), Mark Antony, and Marcus Aemilius Lepidus. The members of the second triumvirate defeated the forces led by Brutus and Cassius at Philippi in 42 B.C. The triumvirate's forces in that battle were led by Mark Antony.

Cleopatra, queen of Egypt, lived in Alexandria, the Egyptian capital city. Mark Antony went to see her, fell in love with her, and remained for a considerable time, much to the disgust of the other two triumvirs. The matter came to a head when Sextus Pompeius, a son of Pompey the Great, became militarily powerful and threatened Rome itself. He maintained his headquarters near Messina (in Sicily); his henchmen were engaged in piracy in and around the Straits of Messina. The pirates become so strong that normal shipping became impossibly dangerous in that area. The three triumvirs met with Sextus Pompeius and offered him the islands of Sicily and Sardinia, if he would cease his piracy of the Straits of Messina and his threat to Rome itself. He agreed.

Later Octavius arrested Lepidus, charging him with treason against Rome. Octavius sailed, with an armada, for Greece and fought a sea battle with Antony near Actium. Octavius won and forced Antony back to Egypt. Finally, Octavius, in Egypt, defeated Antony and added Egypt to the Roman Empire. Antony committed suicide, followed by Cleopatra, thus leaving Octavius as the sole ruler of the Roman Empire.

Master List of Characters

Mark Antony—*Middle-aged protagonist of the play and one of the three members of the second triumvirate of Rome.*

Octavius Caesar—*Triumvir of Rome, the adopted son of Julius Caesar, who became the sole emperor, later known as Caesar Augustus. He was about 20 years younger than Mark Antony.*

Marcus Aemilius Lepidus—*Third member of the second triumvirate.*

Sextus Pompeius (Pompey)—*Son of Pompey the Great, who was one of the three members of the first triumvirate of Rome.*

Cleopatra—*Queen of Egypt, close friend of Mark Antony and previously to Julius Caesar, about 13 years younger than Mark Antony.*

Octavia—*Sister to Octavius and wife to Mark Antony.*

Friends of Mark Antony:
Domitius Enobarbus—*The most important of Antony's friends.*

Ventidius (Ventigius in some manuscripts)—*General under Mark Antony and conqueror of Orodes, King of Parthia.*

Eros—*Former bondservant to Antony, made a free man on the condition that he would kill Antony if Antony requested him to do so; among the most loyal of Antony's friends.*

Scarrus (Scarus in some manuscripts)—*Courageous and trusted soldier under Mark Antony; hero of the war against Octavius Caesar.*

Decretas (Dercetus in some manuscripts)—*Opportunistic soldier and attendant to Antony.*

Demetrius—*Friend of Antony who is worried about Antony's dalliance with Cleopatra and thinks he should attend to his responsibilities as triumvir of Rome.*

Philo—*Friend of Antony and Demetrius; his conversation with Demetrius alerts the audience to what is happening at Cleopatra's court in Alexandria.*

Alexas– *Attendant to Antony and Cleopatra, often Antony's representative at her court during Antony's absence.*

Camidius (Canidius in some manuscripts)—*Lieutenant General to Antony.*

Friends to Octavius Caesar:
Mecenas—*He warns Octavius Caesar against antagonizing Mark Antony.*

Agrippa—*Octavius Caesar's attendant, who was chosen by Octavius as second in line to the throne of the Roman Empire.*

Dolabella—*Ranking attendant of Octavius Caesar.*

Proculeius—*Reluctant participant in Octavius' successful plot to seize Cleopatra after Antony's defeat.*

Thidias—*Attendant of Octavius Caesar and courier between Octavius and Cleopatra after Antony's defeat.*

Gallus—*Octavius Caesar's friend, who speaks little or not at all in the play.*

Towrus ("Tarus" or "Taurus" in some manuscripts)—*Lieutenant General to Octavius Caesar.*

Friends of Sextus Pompeius:
Menas—*A pirate who harasses ships in and near the Straits of Messina, and an officer in Sextus Pompeius' navy.*

Menecrates—*A pirate and an officer of Sextus Pompeius.*

Varrius—*Friend of Sextus Pompeius, he brings news of Antony's expected return to Rome.*

Attendants of Cleopatra:
Charmian—*Cleopatra's closest confidante and attendant.*

Iras—*The next closest confidante of Cleopatra, and the very symbol of loyalty to the queen.*

Seleucus—*Cleopatra's treasurer, whose act of treason near the end of the play infuriates Cleopatra and betrays the great trust she had in him.*

Mardian—*A eunuch and a musician.*

Diomedes—*A distinctly minor character in the play.*

Other Characters:
Silius—*An officer in Ventidius' army, with whom Ventidius converses after the victory over the Parthians.*

Schoolmaster—*Acts as ambassador for Antony to Octavius Caesar.*

Soothsayer (Lamprius in some manuscripts)—*Accurately predicts the future and warns Antony to beware of Octavius.*

Clown—*A misnomer; he brings the deadly asps to Cleopatra near the end of the play and unintentionally produces a period of comic relief before the final tragedy.*

Boy—*A singer who appears only once and sings a few lines.*

Minor Characters:

Messengers, soldiers, attendants, and other minor characters—
*Sometimes identified only with a description (e.g., "Roman,"
"soldier," "servant") without being given a name. When several
characters on the stage answer with one voice, Shakespeare uses
the Latin term "Omnes" to mean "All." Several other characters
are named and appear on stage but do not speak. In some
manuscripts, the Latin term "manet" (remains) and its plural
"manent" (remain) are used to indicate that all on the stage
except these characters exit the stage at that point.*

Summary of the Play

After the battle at Philippi, Antony went to Egypt, and began a
romance with Cleopatra. Messengers from Rome arrive at
Cleopatra's court, demanding Antony's immediate return to Rome
to aid in the fight against Sextus Pompeius and upbraiding him for
his dereliction of the official duties of a triumvir. Antony argues
that he is not needed in Rome, but he does return and marries
Octavius' sister Octavia. A meeting between Pompey (Sextus
Pompeius) and the triumvirs results in a stand-off, in which
Pompey gets the islands of Sicily and Sardinia, in return for ceas-
ing the attack on Rome and the piracy in the Straits of Messina.
Antony and Octavia move to Athens. Later, Octavia, aware a serious controversy is arising between her husband and her brother,
returns to Rome to try to heal the breach.

Octavius, seeking to become the sole emperor, puts Lepidus
in prison and dares Antony to fight him on the sea. Antony, against
the advice of all his advisers, accepts the dare, counting on
Cleopatra's ships to assist him. Cleopatra's ships turn tail and run.
Antony chases the ship carrying Cleopatra and deserts his own
troops at the front, giving Octavius a major victory.

Octavius offers munificent terms of surrender to Cleopatra,
with promises that he has no intention of keeping once he has
taken over Egypt. Dolabella, one of Caesar's henchmen, warns
Cleopatra that Octavius will parade her and her attendants through
the streets of Rome as booty of war.

An angry Antony, wrongly informed that Cleopatra is dead,
tries to commit suicide, but succeeds only in severely wounding

himself. His personal guardsmen carry him to the queen, and he dies in her presence. Cleopatra and her two closest attendants, Charmian and Iras, commit suicide by allowing asps to bite them. Octavius (Caesar) finds the three women dead. He orders a huge state funeral for the pair to be attended by all Octavius' army before he sails for Rome.

Estimated Reading Time

This is one of Shakespeare's longer plays, so reading time should be at least one hour for each of the five acts. Many students will require seven hours for the entire play. This is a play that rewards careful, unhurried reading. Ideally, it should be read in one or two sittings, with occasional referral to the text notes and this study guide, but three or even four sittings is entirely feasible.

Act I

Act I, Scenes 1 and 2

New Characters:

Philo: *friend of Mark Antony*

Cleopatra: *Queen of Egypt*

(Mark) Antony: *triumvir of Rome*

Messenger: *one of several carrying messages between Rome and Egypt. Other messengers appear during the play; none are named*

Demetrius: *friend of Mark Antony*

Charmian: *attendant of Cleopatra and, apparently, the queen's favorite attendant*

Alexas: *friend of Cleopatra and Mark Antony and sometimes the unofficial representative of Antony when he cannot be present at Cleopatra's court*

Soothsayer: *accurately predicts the future and warns Antony to beware of Octavius*

Iras: *attendant of Cleopatra*

(Domitius) Enobarbus: *Roman soldier and friend of Mark Antony*

Mardian: *a eunuch attendant of Cleopatra*

Other attendants, soldiers, etc., sometimes unnamed

Summary

In Scene 1 at Cleopatra's court in Egypt, Demetrius and Philo are discussing the idle behavior of their beloved friend and general. Cleopatra and her attendants enter with Antony. A message arrives from Octavius and Lepidus demanding Antony return and help them in their fight against the son of Pompey the Great. Antony refuses to receive the messengers, but Cleopatra urges him to hear the message. He refuses. She knows that Fulvia (Antony's wife) is a rival, with a greater claim on Antony than she has, even though she is the queen.

In Scene 2, which takes place the next day at Cleopatra's court, the Soothsayer's comments in lines 4 and 5 suggest that Antony will fall before the onslaught of Octavius. The messengers return and deliver their message from Octavius and Lepidus. They demand Antony's return to Rome. Antony learns that Fulvia has died of wounds received in military action.

Analysis

Octavius was not the son of Julius Caesar but rather was the son of his niece. Julius Caesar "adopted" him when he was 18 years old and named him his heir. Shakespeare calls him "Caesar" throughout *Antony and Cleopatra*. In this study guide, he is usually referred to as "Octavius," because he really had not achieved the position of caesar, regardless of his adopted name, until both of the other two triumvirs were dead and he had consolidated the Roman Empire under his rule as emperor.

Shakespeare understood and vividly portrayed the willful and impetuous nature of Mark Antony. Antony had been wildly successful in defeating Brutus and Cassius at Philippi to secure control of the Roman Empire for the triumvirate. Unfortunately, his success at Philippi led to both arrogance and the belittling of aid given to him there by Octavius and by the third triumvir, Lepidus.

Shakespeare considered Lepidus too weak a man to seriously consider as a leader, either military or civil. His actions in the play add to the audience's opinion of him as weak and lacking in personal discipline. The playwright knew that a man lacking in personal discipline was unlikely to be a successful leader on the battlefield or in the halls of government for very long. Lepidus, both in the play and in real life, quickly faded from public view. Even today, most historians consider him to have been a weak leader at best.

Shakespeare's principal characters in this play were real people well known in history. Under such circumstances, there is a limit to how far the playwright can stretch the truth. Antony's impetuosity is obvious in the play; whether he was just as impetuous as a younger man leading the forces of the triumvirate against Brutus and Cassius is a matter of question. What is emphasized is the fact that General Mark Antony, once a man of strong personal discipline, had lost much of that quality through his dalliance with the beautiful Cleopatra. Only near the end of the play, does Antony begin to reassume the figure of the disciplined soldier that marked his younger and most successful years. His fall from his position of near worship by soldiers and friends, visible even in the first few lines of the play, is more than obvious. Near the end of the play he begins to regain their respect.

Although Shakespeare does not specifically say so, he does intimate that Antony's first wife, Fulvia, was much more like Antony was as a young man than as Antony was as an older man resting on his laurels and consorting with Cleopatra. Fulvia supposedly died of wounds received in armed conflict, and that fact serves as a foil to highlight her husband's failure to serve the state in its crisis with Sextus Pompeius. Fulvia had been exiled from Rome because she had participated in a rebellion against the Roman government, but that fact only slightly dulls the foil she provides here. Also important is Antony's reaction to the news of Fulvia's death, and Cleopatra's rather frigid reaction to the same event, in direct violation of Charmian's wise suggestion to her mistress.

The first act constitutes rising dramatic action, as the audience gradually begins to realize that the triumvirs are becoming competitors rather than colleagues, and armed conflict between Antony and Octavius (Caesar) most certainly will result. The alert observer will sense that Lepidus, is not now and never has been a serious factor in the action.

The prophecy of the Soothsayer, of course, is the original clue of how the matter will turn out. This foreshadowing is followed by a dozen less obvious instances. Here we see Octavius ascending and Antony descending, leading to the inevitable triumph of

Octavius. In Scene 2, the Soothsayer's comments suggest that Antony will fall before the onslaught of Octavius—an oblique prophecy here, to be sure, but a valid one. The foreshadowing continues throughout the play. The reference to Herod recalls the fact that he had slaughtered infants in Judea, including, he had hoped, the baby Jesus of Nazareth. Notice also another instance of sarcasm. The overflowing Nile presages not famine, but plenty, because the waters of the Nile are what make the production of food possible in most of Egypt. Without them the nation would be almost entirely a desert, incapable of producing any kind of crops.

Notice the bawdy repartee between Charmian, Alexas, and the Soothsayer at the opening of the scene. Almost every line has sexual overtones, but the references, perfectly plain to an Elizabethan, are much less so to modern readers. "Figs" can refer to the fruit, but also to a penis or an aphrodisiac. Charmian wishes Alexas a wife whom he cannot satisfy sexually, so that she will have 50 other men as lovers. All this is said, of course, in good humor.

The bawdy conversation ends abruptly when Cleopatra enters. Antony's metaphor with "weeds" involves a pun (earing/hearing) in which "earing" means a plant's bearing the "ears" for which it was planted (such as corn). Antony's point is that, just as a blowing wind prevents the growth of some weeds in the fields, so hearing (and appropriate attention to) "news," even if the news is unfavorable, can save us from mistakes later. This metaphor represents a switch in positions for Antony. In Scene 1 he refused to hear the news the messenger brought from Rome. Antony demands an end to the levity. What he must do is both serious and difficult; furthermore, his wife Fulvia is dead.

Later in the act, Shakespeare invokes another pun ("Adiew," after referring to tears and weeping–i.e., dew). Also, here is an example of a metonymy, in which the whole (Egypt) is used for the part (Cleopatra). This usage is commonplace throughout much of the work.

Study Questions

1. Who were the triumvirs who formed the second triumvirate of Rome following the death of Julius Caesar?

2. Why did Mark Antony consider himself at least partially justified in taking an extended "vacation" in Egypt?

3. The Soothsayer in this play performs what function?

4. Mark Antony tends to hold Octavius in contempt. Why? How do we know that he holds such feelings toward Octavius?

5. Why was Octavius so anxious for Mark Antony to return to Rome?

6. Demetrius and Philo perform what extremely important function in the first scene?

7. The Soothsayer carefully absolves himself from causing or even affecting the outcome of events. Why?

8. In Scene 2, Cleopatra says of Antony, "A Roman thought had struck him." In this context, what is a "Roman thought"?

9. Several lines later the messenger says, "The nature of bad news infects the teller." What does he mean?

10. How does Antony learn of Fulvia's death?

Answers

1. The three triumvirs of the second triumvirate were Marcus Aemilius Lepidus, Mark Antony, and Octavius (later called Caesar).

2. In the crucial conflict at Philippi between the triumvirate and the conspiracy led by Brutus and Cassius, Mark Antony led almost all the fighting, whereas Lepidus and Octavius did relatively little for the cause.

3. The Soothsayer prophesies that Octavius will triumph over Mark Antony.

4. Mark Antony still considers Octavius a mere lad; it is beneath Antony's dignity to deal with him. Even Cleopatra refers to Octavius as "scarce-bearded Caesar," and Antony is irritated by the arrival of Octavius' messenger.

5. Sextus Pompeius, who controlled Sicily and whose pirates were raiding ships in the vicinity of the Straits of Messina, had challenged the triumvirate. Octavius considered him a major threat and feared all-out war, in which Antony's expertise would be sorely needed.

6. Their discussion at the beginning of the play informs the audience of Mark Antony's stay in Egypt and of his relationship with the queen, of which they strongly disapprove.

7. The Soothsayer makes it clear that he merely foresees, but he does not cause the events of the future.

8. With surprisingly piercing discernment, Cleopatra identifies a "Roman thought" as a serious thought, presumably as opposed to an "Egyptian thought" which could be frivolous.

9. Messengers bearing bad news often were beaten or otherwise punished, as if they were the cause of the bad news instead of merely the bearer of the tidings.

10. A messenger from Rome brought Antony the news of his wife Fulvia's death.

Suggested Essay Topics

1. Charmian is Cleopatra's servant, but the queen depends heavily on her in several ways. List some of these ways and discuss whether Charmian appeared worthy of such trust.

2. Antony obviously has fallen into considerable lassitude as a result of his relationship with Cleopatra. Are there any indications that Antony might return to the stature he enjoyed as the leader of the triumvirate's forces against Brutus and Cassius at Philippi several years earlier? If so, what are they?

Act I, Scene 3

Summary

Scene 3 takes place later that day in Cleopatra's court. Cleopatra is talking of taunting Antony; Charmian warns her against antagonizing him. Antony enters, talks with Cleopatra and tries to find a way to tell her he must go to Rome, at least for a short time. Suspecting the worst, she accuses him of "treason," although possibly with tongue in cheek. She feigns sickness, hoping to keep him in Egypt and asks him why she should think he'd be true to her when he was false to his wife. Antony has trouble getting even a word in edgewise, as Cleopatra continues her tantrum. Finally he is able to explain that he must return to Rome because his wife is dead. Sextus Pompeius' forces, which hold Sicily, and whose pirates Menas and Menecrates have been terrorizing shipping through the Straits of Messina, is threatening to march on Rome itself.

Grasping hold of herself, Cleopatra assures Antony of her heartfelt love for him, accepts his decision, wishes him Godspeed, and suggests that life will be difficult for her without him.

Analysis

Cleopatra's moods shift (whether truly or feignedly) to the annoyance of Antony. The audience begins to wonder if Cleopatra has the innate ability to love anyone other than herself. Often she acts more like an adolescent girl than like an adult, possibly because she has been a queen for so long, and almost always has her own way. She cannot bear anyone denying her what she wants. When it becomes obvious to her that she cannot control Antony in the same manner as she has controlled her subordinates, she becomes psychologically unsure of herself and attempts to disguise this uncertainty by a bit of bravado. Shakespeare, aware of this tendency in all people (if to a much lesser extent), treats this subject specifically later in the play, when he suggests that people do not know what is truly good for them. The playwright thus foreshadows Cleopatra's apparent mood changes later in the play that surely were an important, if not absolutely definitive, cause for Antony's eventual defeat and destruction.

Study Questions

1. What was Cleopatra's attitude toward Fulvia?

2. Antony says, "I am sorry to give breathing to my purpose." What was his purpose, and what did he mean by giving "breathing" to it?

3. Why was he sorry to have to do that?

4. Cleopatra asks Charmian to "Cut my lace." To what was she referring?

5. Why would she want her "lace" cut?

6. Cleopatra, discussing their relationship with Antony, says, "So Fulvia told me." What did Fulvia tell her, and how?

7. What did Antony mean when he said to Cleopatra, "You'll heat my blood"?

8. Cleopatra says to Antony, "Upon your sword/Sit laurel victory" To what was she referring?

9. Antony refers to Sextus Pompeius as "rich in his father's honour" To what was he referring and in what manner?

10. Cleopatra asks Antony, "Where be the sacred vials thou shouldst fill/with sorrowful water?" To what was she referring?

Answers

1. Cleopatra could not have helped being jealous of Fulvia. To hide her jealously, she taunted Mark Antony about his unfaithfulness to his wife Fulvia and suggested that he would also be unfaithful to her. Her feelings of insecurity caused her to worry about Antony's faithfulness to her.

2. Antony's purpose was to return immediately to Rome. "Giving breathing" to it meant telling his beloved Cleopatra that he was about to leave Egypt for awhile.

3. He was unsure of how the queen would take the news, because she feigned illness to achieve her purposes.

4. Cleopatra indicated that she was about to faint and asked Charmian to cut her bodice.

5. In ancient times, the bodice acted much like a corset might do today; it restricted to some extent the wearer's ability to breathe freely, so cutting it would allow easier breathing.

6. As far as we know, Fulvia and Cleopatra never spoke to each other. Cleopatra is suggesting that Antony will treat her as he treated his wife—by deserting her.

7. Antony meant that Cleopatra would anger him and perhaps force him to lose his temper.

8. The victor's crown was composed of laurel branches and leaves; therefore, Cleopatra is wishing Antony the victor's crown.

9. Sextus Pompeius' father, Pompey the Great, once a member of the first triumvirate of Rome, rebelled against Rome and was destroyed. The comment is bitterly sarcastic.

10. It was customary in Roman times to weep for the dead, catch the tears in "lachrymatory vials," and bury the vials with the dead body. This procedure, were it the emperor who wept, was intended as a great tribute from the emperor to the one who had died.

Suggested Essay Topics

1. In this and the two previous scenes, the character of Antony and Cleopatra is revealed, but Cleopatra is subjected to more character development here than is Antony. Describe, by using specific references from the text, how Shakespeare proceeds to develop Cleopatra's character.

2   Charmian, up to this point, has received about as much character development as has Cleopatra. Based on this and the two previous scenes, suggest how Cleopatra might have acted if Charmian or someone similar to her had not been available. Would Cleopatra's approach to Antony and the

solving of her emotional problems have been different without Charmian? Why, or why not?

Act I, Scenes 4 and 5

New Characters:

Octavius (Caesar): *triumvir of Rome, later to become Augustus Caesar*

Lepidus: *triumvir of Rome*

Summary

Scene 4 takes place at Octavius' house in Rome, before Antony returns from Cleopatra's court. Octavius (Caesar) and Lepidus discuss Sextus Pompeius' challenge. Pompeius' pirates control the Straits of Messina and nearby waters between Sicily and the Italian peninsula. Octavius condemns Antony for his wanton behavior and dereliction of his duties as a triumvir, but Lepidus attempts, weakly, to defend him.

In Scene 5, at Cleopatra's court after Antony's departure to Rome, Cleopatra and her attendants discuss the existing situation. Cleopatra is thinking of Antony so much that even Charmian chides her for doing so. The queen receives Alexas, an emissary from Antony, and promises to write to Antony every day.

Analysis

Scene 4 marks the beginning of a downward spiral for Lepidus that leaves him incapable of any meaningful action, and hence no longer in command of his third of the empire. Later, after Antony has left Rome for Athens, Octavius and Lepidus act in a manner so antagonistic to Antony's interests (by abrogating the treaty with Pompey and launching a military attack on him, and by denigrating Antony in public speeches) that it becomes apparent that the only possible result can be open warfare against Antony.

This scene is the first indication that Octavius is beginning to consider Antony as a rival rather than as a colleague. "Tumble on the Bed of Ptolemy" means "engage in a sexual romp with Cleopatra."

Ptolemy was an earlier husband of Cleopatra but such a close blood relative to her that the marriage would have been of questionable validity, even in ancient Rome. "Rebel to Judgement" means "refuse to abide by one's own common sense and fail to exercise self-discipline." Octavius (Caesar) again comments on Antony's misconduct. It becomes clear that Octavius (Caesar) will use this, and Antony's treatment of Octavia, as a pretext for a military challenge.

In Scene 5, the eunuch Mardian puns on Cleopatra's question "Indeed?" by stating that, because he is a eunuch, he can do nothing "in deed," an example of Shakespeare's frequent bitter humor. Note Cleopatra's comment: "O happy Horse, to bear the weight of Antony!" which validates, to some extent, Charmian's concern that

Cleopatra's constant thought of Antony is overly distracting the queen from other business. Nevertheless, such hyperbole verifies Cleopatra's deep feelings for Antony, even though it causes a titter among the queen's confidantes. Cleopatra loves Antony, whether wisely or otherwise, and challenging that love on the basis that it is not intelligent misses the point. Love, as Shakespeare reminds us time and again throughout his plays, is not to be measured on an intellectual yardstick.

It is obvious by the time Cleopatra promises to write to Antony every day that either she cares deeply for Antony or wants Alexas and her attendants to believe that she does so. Alexas' report of Antony's message to Cleopatra makes it clear that he is devoted to her.

Study Questions

1. Which of the three triumvirs was considered so weak as to be almost totally ineffective?

2. What passage in the first act is our first clue to his weakness and ineffectiveness?

3. At what point in the first act, other than the prophecy of the Soothsayer, do we find foreshadowing of the coming conflict between Mark Antony and Octavius (Caesar)?

4. Cleopatra's feelings toward Mark Antony tend to vary throughout the play. Although she tries to convince him to receive the delegation from Octavius, she finally approves his return to Rome and strongly upbraids her companions for what she considers a derogatory comment about him. What was the comment?

5. Lepidus says, "His faults in him seem as the spots of heaven, / More fiery by night's blackness." About whom does he say this, and what does he mean?

6. Octavius (Caesar) says, in commenting on Antony's sojourn in Egypt, "Let's grant it is not/Amiss to tumble on the bed of Ptolemy." Why would Octavius be so gracious as to comment so about one with whom he is angry?

7. Cleopatra asks Charmian for a drink of mandragora. Why would she desire such a drink?

8. Octavius says to Lepidus, "Pompey/Thrives in our idleness." What did he mean?

9. Menecrates and Menas are called "famous pirates." Later in the play they become relatively important characters. Who are they and in what kind of piracy are they engaged?

10. The messenger says, "the borders maritime/Lack blood to think on't." What did he mean?

Answers

1. Lepidus was considered weak and ineffective, a position that most modern historians agree with.

2. Lepidus weakly defends Mark Antony against Octavius' charges. Lepidus says that Antony was compelled by his nature to act as he did, rather than that he had done so by conscious choice.

3. Octavius, in conversation with Lepidus, refers to Mark Antony as a "great competitor." The word "competitor" in Elizabethan times sometimes meant "partner" but could also hold the connotation that it does today.

4. Charmian refers to the "valiant Caesar." The comment angers Cleopatra, who thinks the comment was intended to refer to Octavius (Caesar). Cleopatra, in a vicious remark, reminds Charmian that it is Mark Antony that is to be honored, not "Caesar."

5. Lepidus makes the comment about Antony, and means that Antony's faults are as minuscule in comparison with his essential greatness as are the stars in comparison with the vastness of the heavens.

6. Octavius knows that Lepidus wants to defend Antony. He does not want Lepidus to think he is totally against Antony, so he throws Antony this sop: The marriage between Cleopatra and Ptolemy would not have been recognized as

valid in Rome because of the close blood relationship between those two. Therefore, Cleopatra could reasonably be
considered as unmarried, and Antony could not be accused
of consorting with a married woman.

7. Mangradora was a narcotic that would cause whoever drinks
    it to fall into a long sleep; thus Cleopatra could pass the time
    until her lover Antony returns to Egypt.

8. Octavius means that Sextus Pompeius (Pompey) is growing
    ever more powerful in his threat to Rome and will continue
    to do so until the triumvirate stops him.

9. Menecrates and Menas are high-ranking soldiers in Sextus
    Pompeius' army, and are commanding pirate ships that are
    devastating maritime commerce in and near the Straits of
    Messina.

10. The messenger means that those living along the Italian
    coast near the Straits of Messina are so terrified of Menecrates
    and Menas that they turn pale whenever they think about
    those two men.

Suggested Essay Topics

1. Scene 4 is, essentially, a conversation between Octavius
    (Caesar) and Lepidus. Both characters will receive much
    more development later in the play. Based on what transpires
    in Scene 4, compare the character and manners of these two
    triumvirs.

2. Alexas is represented in some editions of this play as a ser-
    vant of Antony and in other editions as a servant of
    Cleopatra. He serves throughout the first half of the play as
    a kind of messenger from Antony to Cleopatra when Antony
    is out of the area. Do Cleopatra and her attendants consider
    him Antony's servant and treat him accordingly, or do they
    consider him one of their own? Give examples to support
    your position.

Act II

Act II, Scenes 1 and 2

New Characters:

Pompey: *Sextus Pompeius, son of Pompey the Great, and now the leader of a rebellion against the triumvirate that is sufficiently serious to cause great concern among the triumvirs*

Menecrates: *friend of Pompey*

Menas: *friend of Pompey*

Varrius: *friend of Pompey*

Mecenas: *friend of Octavius. Occasionally confused with Menas*

Agrippa: *friend of Octavius (Caesar)*

Ventidius: *friend of Antony and commander of one of Antony's armies*

Octavia: *sister to Octavius, wife of Antony*

Summary

Scene 1 takes place at Pompey's home in Messina, Sicily. The scene opens with Pompey's men discussing the situation just as the first act opened with Antony's men discussing the situation among themselves before Antony made his appearance.

At the absolute insistence of Octavius, Antony had returned to Rome. Pompey's insurrection was the primary reason that

Octavius and Lepidus wanted Antony back in Rome; Pompey was a real threat and was becoming more so each day. Pompey discusses with his friends the existing military situation concerning his revolt against the triumvirate. Varrius arrives with the news that Antony is expected momentarily in Rome. In a rather arrogant and pompous speech, Pompeius denigrates Antony by calling him an amorous surfeiter, but admits that Antony's "soldiership is twice the other twain" (i.e., twice as competent as that of Octavius and Lepidus combined).

In Scene 2 at Lepidus' home in Rome, Lepidus, in conversation with Enobarbus before the other principals enter, warns Enobarbus to be extremely careful not to stir up any quarrel between Antony and Octavius (Caesar). When Octavius and Antony enter, Lepidus urges them not to let personal differences obscure the purpose for which Antony returned to Rome. Ignoring the plea, Octavius brings up the fact that Fulvia and Antony's brother made war on Octavius. Antony replies he had nothing whatsoever to do with the matter and that they had not asked his advice or permission.

Nevertheless, Antony pays Fulvia a kind of left-handed compliment in saying that she could not be controlled by himself or any other man. He suggests that it would be easier for Octavius to conquer the world than to control Fulvia. At this point, Enobarbus expresses a wish that all men might have wives such as Fulvia, so that the women might go to wars with the men. Here Enobarbus is making a partially sarcastic comment, suggesting that Antony and Octavius are wrangling over relatively trivial matters while a crucial problem faces them. An angry Antony silences his friend and subordinate, Enobarbus, but the soldier still gets in his cut. Octavius replies that he doesn't mind what Enobarbus said but resents the way he said it.

Challenged by Antony to find other grounds for upbraiding him, Octavius accuses Antony of breaking his pledge to come to the aid of the other triumvirs. Here Antony's defense is threefold: (1) his presence in Rome really was not needed earlier, (2) he had been "poisoned" by the beauty of Cleopatra and thus was not in his right mind, and (3) he had indeed returned to Rome as soon as he felt he was needed there. He apologizes for not returning sooner. He receives Lepidus' approval for the apology. Mecenas reminds

the principals that a far more important matter presses for their immediate attention.

Agrippa suggests to seal the friendship of the triumvirs, Antony marry Octavius' sister Octavia; in short order, all agree that this should happen. Enobarbus, in the closing lines of the scene (after the other principals have left the stage), praises the grace and beauty of Cleopatra and says that Antony will never leave Cleopatra, especially for a woman such as Octavia, no matter what formalities (of marriage) might be involved.

Analysis

The second act of *Antony and Cleopatra* continues the rising action begun in the first act. We are introduced to Sextus Pompeius and his staff, against whose as yet sporadic attack the triumvirate is attempting to hold Rome. Sextus, a son of Pompey the Great, is now referred to by the playwright simply as "Pompey," risking confusion with his deceased father. The act opens with Pompey's men discussing the situation among themselves. Shakespeare knew that what the men say among themselves while alone often is notably different than what they say in the hearing of any one or more of the principals. At the absolute insistence of Octavius (Caesar), Antony had returned to Rome. Pompey was a real threat and becoming more so by the day.

Menas' comment, "We are ignorant of our selves," represents a theme that runs through many of Shakespeare's writings, including several plays. Shakespeare seems to be telling us that we don't know what is really good for us and thus we seek goals which in the end, if achieved, would only harm or destroy us.

Sextus Pompeius (Pompey) is far too sure of himself and was certain that Antony would stay in Egypt and be no threat to him. Mark Antony returning to Rome from the court of Cleopatra is a fact that should have greatly alarmed Pompey, but apparently did not. Pompey had acknowledged Antony's "soldiership is twice the other twain." Pompey's arrogance and pomposity come through flagrantly, and the audience has only slight respect for him at this point. The respect increases a bit, though, when he refuses the suggestion of Menas that, while he has a golden opportunity, he murder the triumvirs and seize control of the entire Roman Empire.

Lepidus' primary motivation throughout most of the act is to keep the animosity between Octavius (Caesar) and Antony from destroying the triumvirate, and possibly Rome, too. Perhaps he senses his own inadequacy and realizes that an outright break between Octavius and Antony would destroy him as well. But his efforts are only partly successful, as Octavius and Antony have at it with words, although not yet with weapons. Antony's apology for his late return to Rome reveals a certain humility in his character to balance the arrogance which he sometimes exhibits. It takes all that Lepidus, Mecenas, Agrippa, and Enobarbus can do to bring the conversation back to the principal point—what to do about Pompey. At his wit's end and afraid open warfare might break out between the two triumvirs at any moment, Agrippa proposes marriage between Antony and Octavius' sister, Octavia.

Octavia is offered no real choice in the matter. She is simply a pawn in a political contest. She speaks only a few lines in this act and the next, then permanently disappears from view. Her only real effect on the principals is to give Octavius a perfect excuse for fighting Antony after Antony returns to Cleopatra's court, even though he is married to Octavia.

Perhaps the most important points of *Antony and Cleopatra* are the almost total destruction of Antony's manhood that his dalliance with Cleopatra has produced, the arrogance and pomposity that Pompey has displayed, which inevitably leads to his downfall, and Octavius' desire for personal revenge against Antony that leads to the destruction of many lives in the war in the Ionian Sea and in Egypt. Even the great Octavius wants to proclaim to everyone his "triumph" over his enemies by parading Cleopatra and Antony through the streets of Rome, but not until after he has had his own chance at love-making with Cleopatra. His intentions gradually become known as the play progresses.

Scene 2 portrays the rising conflict between Antony and Octavius (Caesar), which Lepidus tries to quiet. The underlings are acutely aware of this problem, but envision greatly different ways of resolving it. Enobarbus recalls the triumvirs to the problem of what to do about Pompey; Agrippa suggests that a marriage with Octavia might allay the tension. Both approaches are tried; neither works. When Octavia is informed that she is to be married to Antony, she reacts with all the grace of a woman acknowledging her duty and trying to please the triumvirs. Nevertheless, she comes across later as a human pawn in the hands of her brother Octavius.

Study Questions

1. Why did Mark Antony return to Rome from Egypt?

2. What reasons did he give Octavius for not returning sooner?

3. Name two major accusations Octavius brought against Antony.

4. Why was Lepidus anxious to prevent any antagonism between Octavius and Antony from developing?

5. From which character(s), other than Enobarbus, did Lepidus receive the most help in allaying the controversy between the two men?

6. For what comment was Enobarbus severely rebuked by Antony, and why?

7. Why did Agrippa want Octavia to marry Antony?

8. What was Antony's comment about Fulvia when Octavius commented derogatorily on her actions?

9. In the opening Scene of Act II, Menas says: "Know, worthy Pompey/That what they [the great gods] do delay they do not deny." What does Menas mean and what argument does he use to explain why the great gods act as they do?

10. Referring to Silvius, Pompey says, "He dreams." Why does Pompey think Silvius is dreaming instead of accurately reporting the situation?

Answers

1. Octavius and Lepidus, faced with warfare against Sextus Pompeius (Pompey), thought their chances of victory would be greatly increased if Antony were there to command the troops.

2. Antony said that his presence in Rome was not really required earlier than when he actually returned, that Cleopatra's love and charms had intoxicated him, and that he did return to Rome as soon as he thought he really was needed there.

3. Octavius charged Antony with not preventing the rebellion of his wife and his brother against Rome and not fulfilling his vow to come to the aid of the other triumvirs when they needed his aid.

4. Lepidus knew that victory over the rebel Pompey would be much more difficult if Antony and Octavius could not resolve their differences and put up a united front against the common enemy, Pompey.

5. Mecenas politely asked the triumvirs to put aside their differences, and Agrippa proposed marriage between Antony and Octavius' daughter Octavia.

6. Enobarbus told the triumvirs that "You shall have time to wrangle in when you have nothing else to do." Antony considered it wholly inappropriate for a mere soldier to so address his betters (the triumvirs).

7. Agrippa wanted Octavia to marry Antony because he thought such a marriage would solidify the triumvirate and deepen the relationship between Antony and Octavius. The marriage had exactly the opposite effect.

8. Antony said that no man could control Fulvia's actions, not even her husband.

9. Menas reminds his superior, Pompey, that a delay in the gods' answering prayer does not mean their refusal to answer it, and, furthermore, often we ask the gods for things that would harm rather than help us. In such a case, the gods' refusal to answer would be for our own good.

10. Silvius apparently said that Octavius (Caesar) and Lepidus are "in the field," that is, leading an army to attack Pompey. Pompey, however, cannot believe that Antony would leave Cleopatra and Egypt to fight against his forces; he believes without Antony's help, Octavius and Lepidus would be afraid to attack him.

Suggested Essay Topics

1. Contrast the attitude of Antony with that of his friend Enobarbus. Given that Antony is in the power position, discuss any examples that might indicate that Enobarbus was thinking more clearly and intelligently than Antony about the situation in Egypt and in Rome. Had you been Enobarbus, would you have acted and spoken as he did under the circumstances? Why, or why not?

2. Had you been Octavia, how would you have felt about what was transpiring during these two scenes? Would you have felt good about being the wife of a great warrior and triumvir of Rome and the sister of another triumvir? Or would you have preferred to live a much more private life apart from the realms of royalty? Why, or why not?

Act II, Scenes 3, 4, and 5

Summary

Scene 3 takes place in Rome, at the home of Octavius. The Soothsayer who made the oblique predictions in Egypt of Octavius' rise and Antony's fall makes that prediction explicit. He tells Antony that in every instance where he and Octavius are involved in any controversy, Octavius will always win, and he urges Antony to return to Egypt as soon as possible and keep away from Octavius. Antony sends his officer, Ventidius, to Parthia to enter into a campaign that will prove successful and convince the world of the futility of opposing the triumvirate.

Scene 4 takes place on a street of Rome just as the triumvirs are about to leave for the campaign against Pompey in Sicily. Lepidus tells Agrippa and Mecenas that he will be delayed a couple days before he can leave Rome, but that he will meet them in Sicily.

The location of Scene 5 changes abruptly to Cleopatra's palace in Egypt. Alexas is still there, as Antony's unofficial representative during his absence in Rome. Cleopatra jokes with Charmian and Mardian about how she played a trick on Antony and, while he was drunk, dressed him in women's clothes. This forms a bit of comic relief, but a messenger arrives from Rome, and all levity comes to an instant halt. Cleopatra fears that the message is that Antony is dead. Cleopatra queries the messenger and learns that Antony has married Octavia. Furious, she mauls the messenger and orders him whipped. Once she has quieted down, she tries to find out all she possibly can about Octavia and eventually sends Alexas to get a complete physical description of the woman.

Analysis

In Scene 3 it becomes obvious that Octavia is simply to be a "stick" in this play. Her character is not developed sufficiently for her to be considered a major character. The audience could hardly expect her to show much feeling about Antony. After all, the marriage occurred quickly, and she hardly knew her husband. One would suspect that Antony's previous wife, Fulvia, although she does not appear in this play, was a far more interesting and compelling character than was Octavia.

Scene 4 serves merely as a transition scene and adds little or nothing to the plot. It does, however, suggest that Lepidus might have something "in the works" of which the two other triumvirs are unaware. History tells us that such almost certainly was the case, but Shakespeare does not develop that possibility here.

In Scene 5, Cleopatra's mauling and whipping of the messenger represented a practice more or less common in those days. That is one reason why messengers cringed when asked to bear unfavorable news. It illustrates Cleopatra's impetuous, adolescent nature. She acts so even after Charmian, her chief attendant and probably her best female friend, has strongly urged against it. This stubbornness emphasizes even more the fact that Cleopatra is governed by her emotions, almost totally unrestrained by reason.

By this time the audience knows that Cleopatra really loves Antony. Her feelings are what almost any woman would feel under the circumstances—insecurity and jealousy. Those doubts will be allayed later, but for now, she is thoroughly upset.

Study Questions

1. The Soothsayer reappears here. What advice does he give to Antony?

2. Before Ventidius enters, Antony utters a short soliloquy in which he makes two important statements. What are they?

3. In Scene 4, Lepidus says to Agrippa and Mecenas, "Trouble yourselves no further." What, in fact, is he telling these two men?

4. In the opening lines of Scene 5, to what does Cleopatra (humorously) compare Antony?

5. What message does the messenger bring to Cleopatra?

6. Why is Cleopatra afraid to hear the message?

7. With what does Cleopatra threaten the messenger?

8. How does Charmian react to the exchange between the queen and the messenger?

9. What does Cleopatra do after the messenger has exited the stage?

10. Who was the Gorgon Cleopatra mentions near the end of Scene 5?

Answers

1. The Soothsayer urges Antony to return to Egypt and to stay away from Octavius (Caesar); he tells Antony that Octavius

will win over him whenever a contest develops between them.

2. The two statements are that Ventidius must go to Parthia to fight Pacorus (to avenge the murder of Marcus Crassus, a member of the first triumvirate) and that he (Antony) intends to follow the Soothsayer's advice and return more or less permanently to Egypt and Cleopatra.

3. Lepidus is telling them that they need not accompany him to the meeting with Pompey in Sicily—that he will make the journey by himself.

4. Cleopatra compares Antony to fish that she has caught.

5. The messenger from Rome tells Cleopatra that Antony has married Octavia.

6. Cleopatra was afraid that the messenger had brought news of Antony's death.

7. Cleopatra threatens to have the messenger "whipped with wire, and stewed in brine,/Smarting in ling'ring pickle!" Then she threatens to stab him with a knife.

8. Charmian tries to restrain the queen from actions that are totally out of order. Suddenly she realizes that she cannot control Antony as she has been able to control the members of her court.

9. Cleopatra threatens to faint, sends Alexas to learn all he can about Octavia and report back to her, and asks Charmian to lead her to her chamber.

10. The Gorgon, known in legend as Medusa, had her head covered with snakes instead of normal hair. Whoever looked upon her immediately turned to stone.

Suggested Essay Topics

1. Why would Cleopatra want as much personal information about Octavia as she could possibly acquire? Suggest several possible reasons and estimate the validity of each reason. Did she intend to use this information against Octavia? Against Antony? If so, what were her chances of success?

2. In Scene 5, Cleopatra grossly mistreats the messenger who brings her the news that Antony has married Octavia. Discuss the character of Cleopatra as if the only picture you had of her was that offered in Scene 5. Then consider whether this picture of the queen harmonizes with the picture you formed of her from previous scenes (including those in the first act), or whether your picture of Cleopatra has changed substantially from what it was before.

Act II, Scenes 6 and 7

New Character:

Boy: *a singer*

Summary

Scene 6 takes place near Messina, Sicily, where Pompey's ships are anchored. The triumvirate talks with Pompey, hoping to negotiate peace and thus save both sides from losing thousands of men in the fighting. Antony agrees to negotiate with Pompey "on the sea," where Pompey is especially strong, so as not to threaten him during the negotiations.

Both sides have taken some hostages to prevent treachery by either side. The triumvirate has offered Pompey the islands of Sicily and Sardinia if Pompey agrees to call off his pirates and give up his designs on Rome itself. Pompey reminds Antony that Antony is living in Pompey's father's house, which he took without paying for it. Also he mentions the first tryst between Antony and Cleopatra, in which the queen was hidden in a rolled up mattress and brought into Antony's quarters, without anyone else being aware of the matter. Enobarbus, aware that these veiled taunts might break up the meeting and result in all-out war, tries, successfully, to change the subject of the conversation.

Much to the distress of Pompey's henchman, the pirate Menas, Pompey accepts and invites all to his galley for a "state dinner" to seal the agreement. After the principals leave the stage, Enobarbus and Menas discuss the situation, telling each other how they see the matter. They jocularly accuse each other of thievery—Menas on the sea, Enobarbus on the land.

In Scene 7, aboard Pompey's galley in the harbor of Messina, the servants more or less agree that the triumvir Lepidus is pretending to be a much more powerful and wiser man than he actually is. They correctly predict his fall and destruction.

A great deal of drinking takes place, during which Lepidus passes out and must be carried to shore. Menas suggests quietly to Pompey that the cable that holds the boat near the Italian shore be surreptitiously cut, so that the boat will drift away from shore, and that he murder all three triumvirs; then Pompey might be able to take over the entire Roman Empire without significant loss of life. Pompey refuses, but tells Menas that he should have done it without asking permission—a permission that Pompey must refuse or sacrifice his honor: the triumvirs were Pompey's guests. Menas, in an aside, says that opportunity once spurned never returns again, and thus foreshadows the fall of Pompey.

During the scene, Menas and Enobarbus reveal their feelings about the matter—feelings that hardly do honor to the principals. Menas is sullen, sure that Pompey has made a tragic mistake in handling the situation the way he has. Enobarbus, on the other hand, is quite jovial. The scene ends with the end of the dinner and a drunken dance in honor of Bacchus, the Greek god of wine.

Analysis

In Scene 6, "Sails" means "ships," the same substitution appears again in Act III. Enobarbus says that Antony will return to Cleopatra and forsake Octavia, who is "of a holy, cold and still conversation." He refers to Cleopatra as Antony's "Egyptian dish," a rather startling metaphor.

In Scene 7, the servants correctly predict Lepidus' fall and destruction. This is only one of many places in Shakespeare's plays in which the conversation of unnamed minor characters validly predicts the future. Notice the simile concerning the crocodile; Shakespeare normally uses metaphor more frequently than he does simile. A great deal of drinking takes place, during which Lepidus, passes out and must be carried to shore. This is another in the series of events that depict Lepidus' character—lack of personal discipline and self-control—that lead inexorably to his destruction.

Menas suggests that opportunity, once spurned, never returns again. He thus predicts the eventual downfall of Pompey. Unexplained is how the murder of the triumvirs without Pompey's foreknowledge would have spared him any dishonor. The host is generally considered responsible for the conduct of his servants and staff. No mention is made of what would happen to the hostages in such a case.

Notice the onomatopoeia, "Plumpy," in line 108 where the word sounds like one meaning for which the word is often used. As the revelry ends, the audience knows that Octavius will triumph and become, in truth, Caesar, and that Pompey, Lepidus, and Antony, are on their downward spirals.

Study Questions

1. Did Menas exhibit strong confidence in Pompey's actions in accepting the triumvirate's offer of peace?

2. In the opening line of Scene 6, Pompey says, "Your hostages I have, and so have you mine." What are the hostages and why would Pompey and the triumvirate have them?

3. Explain why Antony, in Scene 6, tells Pompey that "Thou canst not fear us."

4. When Menas and Enobarbus, alone on the stage after the others have exited, discuss the situation, of what do they accuse each other?

5. To whom was Octavia married before she married Mark Antony?

6. What is Enobarbus' opinion of the marriage between Antony and Octavia?

7. Antony says to Octavius (Caesar), "They take the flow o'th'Nile/By certain scales i'th'Pyramid." What is he talking about?

8. Antony says, "These quicksands, Lepidus,/Keep off them, for you sink." Of what "quicksands" is Antony warning Lepidus?

9. Near the end of Scene 6, a most unusual conversation occurs between Pompey and Enobarbus. What are they discussing?

10. What incident indicates Pompey's desire to become the ruler of the world?

Answers

1. Menas thought Pompey was making a great mistake by acceding to the peace offer the triumvirs had made.

2. To prevent either party from gaining an advantage over the other while they are discussing the possibilities of peace, each warring faction takes one or more hostages, usually relatively high-ranking people, belonging to the other side.

3. It was generally recognized that Pompey's forces were superior on the sea, but the triumvirate's forces were superior on the land. Antony offers to hold the talks at sea—an advantage to Pompey.

4. They accuse each other, only partly in fun, of being thieves.

5. Octavia was married to Caius Marcellus, a major Roman official.

6. Enobarbus says Antony will return to his "Egyptian dish" (Cleopatra), regardless of his marriage to Octavia, and that will cause a falling out between Octavius (Caesar) and Antony.

7. Antony is explaining that markings on the pyramid indicate how deeply the Nile River has overflowed its banks.

8. Antony is warning Lepidus, his fellow triumvir, of the dangers of consuming too much alcohol. Lepidus does not heed the warning and drinks so much that he passes out.

9. Pompey and Enobarbus are discussing the manner in which Antony first met Cleopatra. She was wrapped in a carpet and carried to Antony's quarters, so that nobody would know about the meeting.

10. When Menas suggests that he kill all three triumvirs and thus deliver the world to Pompey, Pompey tells him that he should have done so without asking, but now Pompey must refuse permission or violate the standards of hospitality and thus dishonor himself.

Suggested Essay Topics

1. Write a personal portrait of Pompey, comparing or contrasting (1) Pompey's view of himself, (2) the triumvirs' view of him, (3) his associates' and friends' view of him, and (4) history's view of him.

2. History has considered Lepidus the weakest member of the second triumvirate. Summarize how Shakespeare portrays his weakness, then indicate some reasons why historians have considered him weak. Was his weakness the result of his personal failings or of circumstances over which he had no control? Why?

3. If Menas had simply murdered the three triumvirs and then told Pompey that he had done so, how would Pompey have handled the situation? How would he have preserved his "honor" in the view of the world?

Act III

Act III, Scene 1

New Character:

Silius: *friend of Antony and soldier in Antony's army commanded by Ventidius*

Summary

Scene 1 takes place in Syria, probably on a plain near the battlefield. Ventidius, commanding Mark Antony's army, has won a significant battle against Orodes, king of Parthia. His troops bear the body of Pacorus, Orodes' son, as a symbol of victory. (The battle constituted revenge against the Parthians for the treacherous murder of Marcus Crassus, a member of the first triumvirate of Rome.) Ventidius is urged to pursue his triumph to conquer adjacent regions, but he refuses, citing the danger of promoting himself and possibly eclipsing his general, Antony. Doing that has proved dangerous before with other generals, and Ventidius wants no part of that here. He has done his duty and is ready to return home, but he wants Antony to understand that his army was so successful because they were well paid and well cared for, something that could not be said for many armies of that day.

Analysis

This act illustrates the point where rising action ends and falling action begins. In most Shakespearean plays that point occurs somewhere in the third act, with two acts yet to follow. That is a contrast to the situation in modern drama, where rising action usually continues until later in the play—often to somewhere in the final act. In *Antony and Cleopatra*, surprises continue to occur until the very end of the play, but the final outcome is not in doubt after Act III.

Nevertheless, different commentators could reasonably place the "climax" of this play at any of several other points: (1) at the point where Antony again, at least temporarily, regains his status as a great military leader, (2) at the point where he commits suicide, (3) at the point where Cleopatra commits suicide (and the rather unusual manner in which she does so), or (4) at the point where Octavius (Caesar), deprived of his goal to parade Cleopatra through the streets of Rome as a captive, orders a large state funeral for them and grants Antony's last wish—to be buried with Cleopatra in her tomb.

The third act emphasizes a major message of *Antony and Cleopatra*, that many a man has been ruined when he allowed his love (or infatuation) for a woman to overrule his better judgment and destroy both his stature and his life and cause. Women are the heroines of Shakespeare's plays about as often as they are villains, but they are often portrayed as pawns for men to push around on a giant chessboard. An example of this in the play is Octavia, who has no reasonable choice but to accept her brother's decision to marry her to Antony.

In *Antony and Cleopatra*, as in so many of his other plays, Shakespeare portrays the tragic results of letting one's emotions overpower the intellect. But, as the playwright well knew, the tendency to allow one's heart to rule one's head is endemic in the human race, as it always has been since the beginning of recorded history.

Study Questions

1. Why was Antony so anxious to conquer Parthia and its king, Orodes?

2. What particular function does Silius perform in this scene?

3. What did Silius want Ventidius to do?

4. Why did Ventidius refuse to do it?

5. What did Ventidius plan to do immediately after his victory?

6. What was the most pressing message Ventidius intended to send to Antony, other than informing him of the victory, and why was that message of supreme importance?

7. Ventidius says, "Caesar and Antony have ever won/More in their officer than person." What did he mean?

8. Who was Sossius?

9. Silius says, "Thou hast, Ventidius, that/Without the which a soldier and his sword/Grants scarce distinction." Is this a complimentary or a disparaging remark to Ventidius, and why?

10. What figure of speech does Ventidius' use of the word "horse" in line 34 represent, and what is its meaning?

Answers

1. Antony was anxious to avenge the Parthians' treacherous murder of Marcus Crassus, a member of the first triumvirate of Rome.

2. Silius is a "stick" who serves as a foil to allow Ventidius to explain to the audience what had transpired in Parthia and why it was important.

3. Silius wanted Ventidius to follow the fleeing Parthians, capture more territory, and win more honors for Antony.

4. Ventidius knew from his study of military history that subordinate generals who outshine their superior officers often are destroyed by those officers to prevent any chance that the subordinate should supplant the top general.

5. Ventidius planned to go to Athens to communicate to Antony his victory over Parthia.

6. Ventidius wanted to emphasize that his troops won the great victory because they were well paid and carried the banners

of the famous General Antony. The distinct implication is that, had the troops not been well paid and well treated by their generals, they quite likely would not have won the victory.

7. Ventidius meant that both Antony and Octavius (Caesar) had been more successful when their subordinates commanded their armies in actual conflict than when they had commanded the armies themselves.

8. Sossius, a commander of roughly the same rank as Ventidius, made the mistake of winning too many great honors for himself, and thus lost his general's favor.

9. Silius is complimenting his commander, Ventidius, by saying that Ventidius possesses the discretion without which a commander is little more than a walking sword.

10. "Horse" is a synecdoche, in which the part (horse) represents the whole (the Parthian cavalry).

Suggested Essay Topics

1. Ventidius was afraid that if he conquered more territory than Antony had told him to, Antony might have been displeased and might have punished Ventidius. Based on what you have learned thus far about Antony, was Ventidius' fear justified? Why, or why not?

2. Orodes, king of Parthia, treacherously murdered Marcus Crassus, a member of the first triumvirate of Rome. In your opinion, did the circumstances surrounding the death of Crassus justify the invasion of Antony's army under the command of Ventidius and the killing of the king's son Pacorus? Why, or why not?

Act III, Scenes 2, 3, and 4

Summary

In Scene 2 at Octavius' house in Rome, Agrippa and Enobarbus are discussing Lepidus. They comment about how greatly Lepidus

loves Octavius (Caesar), how greatly he loves Antony, and then on which he loves more. Octavia and her husband Antony are taking leave of Octavius, enroute to Athens. Octavius weeps at the parting; Octavia is his sister, and he is concerned for her welfare. Octavius' lines tell Antony that he does not trust him. Antony asks Octavius not "to offend him with distrust," but Octavius does not back down. Octavia cannot reconcile her emotions with her speech, as Antony himself points out. Antony and Octavia depart for Athens.

Scene 3 takes place at Cleopatra's palace in Alexandria. Cleopatra, overcome with insecurity now that she has a real rival in Octavia, tries to find out as much as she can about Antony's new life and especially about Octavia. The messenger from Rome has seen Octavia and tries to answer Cleopatra's questions. The comments of those with the queen, however, tend to be directed to what they think will please her, rather than to what the actual situation is.

In Scene 4 at Antony and Octavia's house in Athens, Antony is angry that Octavius (Caesar) has undertaken action against Pompey without consulting Antony and without his help, thus breaking the treaty the triumvirs made with Pompey. Also, he is furious that Antony has published his "will" for the Roman people to hear. The will credits Antony with precious little kindness. He has given little or no credit to Antony in his speeches to the citizens of Rome. Octavia, seeing a potential conflict developing between her husband and her brother, seeks to go to Rome and reconcile the two men before full-scale war breaks out between them. Antony grants Octavia's wish to return to Rome.

Analysis

In Scene 2, the net effect of the discussion between Agrippa and Enobarbus is to denigrate Lepidus, his dwindling status heightened by how extravagantly he pours praises on the other two triumvirs.

In Scene 3, no direct comparison is made between Cleopatra's beauty and that of Octavia; the scene portrays Cleopatra's jealousy, but also suggest that Cleopatra's love for Antony is, after all, real.

In Scene 4, Antony's anger that Octavius (Caesar) has undertaken action against Pompey without consulting Antony and without his help, and that Antony has published his "will," for all practical purposes, cements the fact that war between the two men is imminent. Antony grants Octavia's wish to return to Rome, probably because he knows armed conflict is to ensue, and he wants to spare Octavia. In this case, his desire to spare his wife, Octavius' sister, is at least as much a motivation as his desire to be with Cleopatra. Antony is still fully capable of selfless thought of others, whether they deserve such magnanimity, as did Octavia, or whether they don't.

Study Questions

1. Who are Agrippa and Enobarbus discussing in Scene 2?

2. Why does Lepidus praise both Octavius and Antony?

3. Why does Octavius weep when Antony and Octavia leave?

4. Where are Antony and Octavia going?

5. Whom does Octavius express his distrust of?

6. What mission does Cleopatra give her messenger?

7. Why is Cleopatra concerned about Octavia?

8. In Scene 4, Why is Antony angry at Octavius?

9. Why does Octavia wish to go to Rome?

10. Why does Antony grant Octavia's wish?

Answers

1. Enobarbus and Agrippa are discussing Lepidus.

2. Lepidus praises both Octavius and Antony because of his own dwindling status.

3. Octavius weeps out of concern for Octavia's welfare.

4. Octavia and Antony are departing for Athens.

5. Octavius expresses his distrust of Antony.

6. He is sent to gather information on Octavia.

7. Cleopatra sees Octavia as her rival and is jealous of her.

8. Antony is angry because Octavius has taken action against Pompey without consulting him.

9. Octavia wishes to go to Rome to reconcile the differences between her brother and Antony.

10. Antony grants her wish because he fears a full-scale war is imminent.

Suggested Essay Topics

1. Agrippa and Enobarbus, in Scene 2, discuss whether Lepidus loves Octavius more than Antony or Antony more than

Octavius. The discussion distinctly denigrates Lepidus, also a triumvir of Rome. Does his conduct in the play justify the ridicule offered by these two soldiers? Why, or why not?

2. In Scene 4, Antony is explaining to Octavia how her brother Octavius has wronged him. Do these accusations appear to you to justify Antony's anger with Octavius? Why or why not?

Act III, Scenes 5, 6, and 7

New Characters:

Eros: *friend and servant of Mark Antony*

Towrus: *second in command of Octavius' army*

Camidius (Canidius): *second in command of Antony's army*

Summary

In Scene 5 at Antony's house in Athens, somewhat later in the day than the previous scene, Enobarbus and Eros discuss the existing political situation, primarily as it concerns Octavius and Antony. Octavius has seized and imprisoned Lepidus—that after the two triumvirs had fought a successful campaign against Pompey.

Scene 6 takes place in Rome, just after Octavia has arrived from Athens. Octavius (Caesar) receives Octavia and tells her that Antony has greatly wronged her and has enlisted the help of many nations in a forthcoming war against him—a considerable overstatement at best. Octavius is angry with Antony for not providing a sufficient escort for so great a woman as Octavia—a totally invalid charge, because Antony had offered her as much of an escort as she desired.

In Scene 7 at Antony's camp in Actium, Greece, Enobarbus and Cleopatra discuss the situation. Enobarbus urges Cleopatra to return to Egypt. He explains that she will distract Antony's attention from the crucial matter at hand—defeating Octavius (Caesar) if a battle ensues. In an analogy, he says that a stallion cannot properly devote himself to his master and rider if there are mares in the pasture with him. The stallion, even with the rider on his back, will mount the mare if she is in heat. But Cleopatra refuses to abide by his advice and insists on not only being with Antony but also in having her navy attack Octavius and precipitate a sea battle. Octavius soon will dare Antony to fight him on the sea.

The news arrives that Octavius has quickly crossed the Ionian Sea and taken the city of Toryne, to the amazement of Antony, who could hardly believe that he had crossed so quickly to Greece. After Antony refuses to reconsider his rash decision to fight Octavius on the sea, a soldier swears by Hercules that his efforts to dissuade Antony from a sea battle were valid and correct. Camidius, Antony's second in command, agrees with the soldier.

Analysis

In Scene 5, Octavius seized and imprisoned Lepidus—after the two triumvirs had fought a successful campaign against Pompey. Historians tell us that Lepidus did turn against Octavius in the war against Pompey, but Shakespeare neither mentions nor alludes to that fact anywhere in this play. Had he done so, the imprisonment of Lepidus could be considered to be at least somewhat justified. Shakespeare's contempt for Octavius (Caesar) gradually becomes evident. Perhaps it was to engender such contempt among the audiences of his day that the playwright omits this important detail. If so, it is another example of the manner in which Shakespeare "adjusts" the known facts of history to suit his purposes, which usually, but not always, heightens the dramatic effect of the action on stage.

Scene 6 yields more such examples of Octavius' attempts to belittle Antony in the eyes of everyone else, including his own sister, Octavia. Octavius' telling Octavia that Antony has greatly wronged her and has enlisted the help of many nations in a forthcoming war against him is a considerable overstatement at best. At worst, it is an outright lie. The intended effect is to make Octavia feel sorry for herself (more than she already does) and convince her what a scoundrel Antony really is. Octavius' misstatement of the situation is a forewarning of his less than pure motives for whatever he does. Octavius' anger with Antony for not providing a sufficient escort for so great a woman as Octavia is groundless. Antony had offered her as much of an escort as she desired.

In Scene 7, Cleopatra's insecurity probably precipitates her highly unwise decision not to return to Egypt and allow Antony to fight Octavius (Caesar) without having to think about her. She apparently felt she could not take a chance on being away from Antony any longer than absolutely necessary. Furthermore, she thought that her offer of her navy would serve to solidify their relationship.

Antony foolishly and with far too much pride accepts Octavius' dare to fight a sea battle, and thus seals his own doom and that of Cleopatra. His disregard of all the efforts by seasoned commanders and soldiers to dissuade him from a sea battle leads to the understanding that Antony will be utterly destroyed. The synecdoche "sails" (the part) meaning "ships" (the whole) appears for the second time in this play. (A synecdoche, in which the part stands for the whole, is the opposite of a metonymy, in which the whole stands for the part.)

Antony claimed to be a descendant of Hercules, a mythical Greek hero who had become a demigod. Hercules had won a significant victory (against Antaeus) while standing on land. When Hercules, however, later put himself into the power of a woman, he was destroyed. This supposed tie between Hercules and Antony, well known to many of Antony's day, explains several events that occur later.

Study Questions

1. What is learned in Scene 5 about what happened to Lepidus?

2. Why was Octavius angry with Octavia when she returned to Rome?

3. Octavius blamed Antony for this lack of courtesy to Octavia, but was it Antony's fault?

4. Why does Octavius tell Octavia to turn against her husband?

5. Why does Enobarbus, in Scene 7, attempt to get Cleopatra to return from Actium (in Greece) to Egypt?

6. It appears that Octavius is looking for ways to justify his defeat and capture of Antony. Why would he want to do that?

7. Why does Antony decide to fight Octavius (Caesar) at sea?

8. Camidius says, "His whole action grows/Not in the power on't. So our leader's led,/And we are women's men." What is the meaning of this statement?

9. Who is Towrus?

10. What are the "rotten planks" to which the soldier refers in line 62 of Scene 7?

Answers

1. Lepidus, having helped Octavius (Caesar) in the war against Pompey, has been imprisoned in Rome by Octavius.

2. Octavius was angry that Octavia had not come to him with a full retinue of servants and a great deal of fanfare.

3. It was Octavia's fault, not Antony's, that she did not have such a retinue. Antony had offered it, but Octavia had refused it.

4. Octavius told his sister Octavia that Antony had left Athens and gone to Egypt to be with Cleopatra and that Antony had enlisted the aid of several kings to fight against Octavius .

5. Enobarbus, rightly fearing that Cleopatra's presence would distract Antony from his military duties, tried to persuade Cleopatra to return to Egypt, at least until the battles were over.

6. Octavius wanted to be the sole emperor of Rome; to become such, he had to get rid of Antony as he had gotten rid of Lepidus. A lesser motive was to seize Cleopatra and parade her through Rome as a prize of war.

7. Antony did not want to fight a land battle until he had won a sea battle, because Octavius had dared him to fight at sea. Secondarily, Antony wanted to please Cleopatra by using her fleet in the battle.

8. The soldier observes that Antony's decisions are not based on an honest evaluation of his real sources of strength, and that his forces are being governed, in the last analysis, by women, a statement severely derogatory to Antony.

9. Towrus is the general who is to command the forces of Octavius (Caesar) in the forthcoming battle with Antony.

10. The "rotten planks" constitute a synecdoche for "ships."

Suggested Essay Topics

1. Octavius has deposed Lepidus from his place on the trium-
    virate and imprisoned him in Rome. Some historians tell us
    Lepidus joined Pompey in making war on Octavius, but
    Shakespeare does not mention that matter. If Lepidus had
    been guilty of such treason, the actions taken against him
    would have been justified. Were they justified on the basis
    of what Shakespeare tells us in this play? Why, or why not?

2. Why do you think Cleopatra refused to return to Egypt from
    Greece when Enobarbus strongly suggested that she do so?
    What reasons, if any, did she offer for deciding to stay in
    Greece while Antony fought the battle? What was her real
    reason for staying?

Act III, Scenes 8-11

New Character:

Scarrus: *Roman soldier and friend of Mark Antony*

Summary

Scene 8 takes place in Greece near Actium. Octavius warns his commander, Towrus, not to strike Antony by land until after the battle at sea. The future of the conflict depends on this battle plan. Nearby, in Scene 9, Antony gives some military orders to Enobarbus concerning the placement of troops so that the sea battle can be observed.

In Scene 10 , which takes place at Actium, several hours later, Enobarbus and Scarrus discuss the total rout of the ships. All of Cleopatra's navy has turned tail and run southward toward Peloponnesus and the battle appears lost. Even loyal Scarrus says that Antony's actions in chasing after Cleopatra's ship was an unparalleled act of cowardice and dereliction of duty, unequaled in any war. Camidius enters and confirms the disaster.

In Scene 11, Antony leaves his forces and chases after Cleopatra, who is aboard her fleeing flagship. Eventually he catches her. It is not certain whether the reunion occurs in Egypt or on the Peloponnesus, but the latter seems more probable. In total dejection, and ashamed of himself for chasing Cleopatra and her navy instead of remaining with his men, he advises his soldiers to give up and go to Octavius (Caesar). Cleopatra's attendants urge her to comfort Antony, which she does. Antony tells those soldiers faithful to him to take the ship laden with gold which Antony had reserved for himself, and go to make their peace with Octavius (Caesar). Then he accuses Cleopatra of treachery. She pleads for forgiveness, and says she never thought Antony would try to follow her. Antony replies that she should have known he'd follow her (to the ends of the earth, if need be). Nevertheless, Cleopatra's protestations of innocence have their effect, and Antony ceases his verbal attack on her.

Analysis

The statement in Scene 8, in which Octavius tells his commander not to begin land action against Antony until after the sea battle, indicates how thoroughly Octavius is counting on the sea battle, a type of fighting in which Antony lacks experience to win the war. Scene 9 serves simply as a transition scene, in which Antony gives some orders about the placement of troops.

In Scene 10, however, Enobarbus and Scarrus discuss the total rout of the ships. At this point the audience learns of Antony's disastrous defeat, which they were, or at least should have been, expecting. The appearance of Camidius confirms the scope of the disaster. Antony foolishly accepted a dare that put him and his troops at a severe disadvantage; he did not deserve to win.

In Scene 11, Cleopatra's excuse for running away is invalid; it in no way mitigates her cowardice (and immaturity) in allowing her ships to turn tail and run from the battle. But Antony's reply that she should have known he'd follow her is an equally invalid excuse on his part. The truth of the matter is that she should not have run away, and that, even if she did run away, he should never have chased her while the battle was still raging. It is a sad indication of how far Antony has fallen from his once lofty status as one of the world's most competent soldiers.

Study Questions

1. What instructions did Octavius give his general, Towrus?

2. Why did he decide to so instruct Towrus?

3. What is the first indication that Antony has lost this battle?

4. Why did Antony leave his men and go in search of Cleopatra?

5. What decision does Camidius, Antony's commander, make?

6. What instructions does Antony give after the battle is lost?

7. What sad comment does Antony make about himself?

8. Does Antony blame Cleopatra for his defeat?

9. How does she reply to his comments? Are the replies justified?

10. How does Antony react to her comments?

Answers

1. Octavius (Caesar) tells Towrus not to begin a land battle against Antony until the sea battle is finished.

2. Octavius knew that Antony had far more power on the land than on the sea; therefore, it was highly to Octavius' advantage to fight Antony on the sea rather than on the land.

3. The first indication of Antony's defeat comes in Scene 10, where Enobarbus says that the Egyptian admiral, with all his ships, has turned tail and fled from Octavius' forces.

4. Antony is afraid that Cleopatra has left him permanently, and he wants to get her back. He is so upset that he deserts his own forces to follow her.

5. Canidius resolves to desert Antony and to take his soldiers and defect to Octavius (Caesar).

6. Antony tells his soldiers to take the gold Antony has hidden in his ship in the harbor, to divide it among themselves, and to defect to Octavius.

7. Antony tells his soldiers that he has lost his way forever and that he has lost command.

8. Antony, at least partly, blames Cleopatra for his defeat. The cowardice of the queen's admirals and sailors was totally inexcusable.

9. Cleopatra says she had no idea that Antony would follow her instead of remaining at the battle site continuing to lead his men. The reply is justified only to the extent that she probably thought Antony too much a man to desert his troops in the heat of battle

10. Antony apparently accepts her apology; they kiss, and he calls for wine and food.

Suggested Essay Topics

1. In the first sea battle of the war between Antony and Octavius (Caesar), Cleopatra's ships turn tail and flee from the battle, granting Octavius the victory. Why do you think they fled? There is no record in this play that they were seriously defeated in the open sea battle, and history leaves the point in question. Could Cleopatra not control her sea captains? Or was it Cleopatra that gave the order to flee? Why do you think they gave up without mounting a serious fight? Can you find any clue in the play itself as to why such an unexpected thing might have happened, especially after Cleopatra had pledged her navy to Antony's aid? Or is the matter simply one of abject cowardice on the part of the naval commanders and sailors?

2. Was Antony's commander, Camidius, in any way justified in defecting, with his troops and cavalry, to Octavius (Caesar), or was it simply another example of cowardice on the part of Camidius? If you had been one of Camidius' soldiers, how would you have felt about the surrender and defection to Octavius? Would you have gone along with Camidius and defected to Octavius, or would you have held out to serve Antony (assuming you were given that opportunity)? How would you have justified your choice, regardless of which choice you made?

Act III, Scenes 12 and 13

New Characters:

Dolabella: *friend of Octavius (Caesar)*

Thidias: *friend of Octavius*

Summary

Scene 12 takes place at Octavius' camp. Antony has sent his children's schoolmaster to Octavius—perhaps a final insult to the victor, whom Antony always has called a mere boy. The emissary asks that Antony be allowed to live in Egypt, or, if not Egypt, as a private man in Greece. Cleopatra agrees to submit to Octavius' rule. Octavius refuses to grant Antony's request but gives the emissary a favorable answer to Cleopatra, providing only that she drive Antony from Egypt or kill him. Then he sends his own emissary, Thidias, to Antony and Cleopatra. Thidias is authorized to offer Cleopatra any terms he thinks appropriate.

Scene 13 takes place at Cleopatra's palace in Alexandria, where she and Antony have returned following the disastrous sea battle. After Antony's defeat, Cleopatra asks Enobarbus, "Is Antony or we at fault for this?" "Antony," Enobarbus answers, for Antony would "make his Will Lord of his Reason."

Antony, aware of Octavius' terms that the price of Cleopatra's safety is his own destruction, writes Octavius a letter, challenging him to a sword duel to settle the matter, rather than destroy thousands of soldiers in a final battle. Thidias arrives and tells Cleopatra that Octavius knows that she took up with Antony through fear of him, not love of him.

Antony returns and orders Thidias whipped—another sign that he lets his emotions control his intellect. Then he asserts his will to continue the war: "I am Antony yet," after which he obliquely accuses Cleopatra of acting like a whore: "Would you mingle Eyes With one who ties his [Octavius Caesar's] Points?" In a famous speech she defends herself and satisfies Antony, who now plans a final military and naval attack on Octavius. Antony proposes a feast, to which Cleopatra agrees, reminding him that it is her birthday.

Analysis

In Scene 12 Antony has insulted Octavius (Caesar) by sending his children's schoolmaster to Octavius, whom Antony always has called a mere boy. (At this point, in 31 B.C., Octavius was 32 years old; Antony was 51.) It is evident that Octavius has no intention of abiding by his own or Thidias' promises to Cleopatra. All he desires is physical possession of Cleopatra. Shakespeare, never an admirer of Octavius Caesar, paints a vivid picture of his lack of character.

In Scene 13, when Cleopatra asks Enobarbus which person was at fault in the defeat, the playwright makes a point which is made many times in his plays: that every man is responsible for his own actions. When Octavius tells Cleopatra that he knows she took up with Antony out of fear of him, not out of love for him, he offers Cleopatra an "out." However, Octavius' "gracious" comment is not valid; Cleopatra did not submit to Antony through fear. Nevertheless, Cleopatra accepts his statement as true, displaying her own weakness—a weakness which she bemoans later in the play.

When Antony returns to the scene and orders Thidias whipped, the audience sees another indication that Antony lets his emotions control his intellect. Nevertheless, his statement, "I am Antony yet," and his willingness to continue the war, suggest that the old (and real) Antony is returning to the stage. At this point, Cleopatra's stature, too, takes a turn for the better. ("But since my lord is Antony again, I will be Cleopatra.")

Study Questions

1. Whom does Antony send as an emissary to Octavius (Caesar)? Why?

2. What response does Octavius give the emissary?

3. When Antony challenges Octavius to a sword duel to settle the matter between them, does he believe Octavius will accept the challenge? Why?

4. What is Enobarbus' opinion of Antony's challenge to Octavius?

5. What action does Enobarbus contemplate as a response to Antony's challenge to Octavius?

6. Why does Antony order the servants to whip Thidias?

7. Did Thidias ask for mercy during the whipping?

8. Who was the "Caesarion" that Cleopatra mentions in her response to Antony's charge that she is, for practical purposes, simply a whore?

9. What is Antony's response to Cleopatra's impassioned answer to his charge?

10. How does Enobarbus react to this response?

Answers

1. Antony sends his schoolmaster as an emissary to Octavius (Caesar), probably as a slap at Octavius, whom Antony considers to be a mere lad.

2. Octavius says he has no ears for Antony's plea, but, if Cleopatra will kill or banish Antony, her plea will be heard.

3. Antony is not thinking clearly at this point; otherwise, he would have realized the futility of his offer. Octavius would be a fool to accept the challenge, but Antony, in his confused state of mind, probably thought there was a reasonable possibility that he would accept it.

4. Enobarbus, to this point one of the most loyal of Antony's friends and soldiers, thinks that Antony has lost his power of judgment by offering to fight a duel with Octavius (Caesar).

5. Enobarbus is beginning to consider deserting Antony and defecting to Octavius.

6. Whipping an emissary is the ultimate insult to the person who sent the emissary. Antony wants to show his utter contempt for Octavius.

7. At some point during the whipping, Thidias did "ask favour" (beg for a pardon).

8. The Caesarion was a son Cleopatra had born to Julius Caesar years before. Octavius (Caesar) had him killed, thus eliminating a possible challenge to himself as the emperor.

9. Antony says he is satisfied with Cleopatra's answer, informs her that he will attack Octavius' forces, and suggests a massive banquet for his own and her forces.

10. Enobarbus is disgusted with Antony and begins to make plans to defect to Octavius.

Suggested Essay Topics

1. Enobarbus, a loyal supporter of his friend and commander Antony, becomes disillusioned with Antony's leadership. What were the options open to Enobarbus? Which ones did he choose, what were the results, and were these results inevitable, given the choices he makes?

2. Whipping messengers who brought bad news was common in the period of which Shakespeare wrote. If you had been Thidias, how would you have handled the matter? If you had been Antony, would you have had Thidias whipped? Why, or why not? If you had been Octavius, how would you have reacted when his messenger Thidias returned, bearing the welts resulting from the whipping? Did the whipping of Thidias have any material effect on the final outcome of the battle between Antony's forces and those of Octavius (Caesar)?

Act IV

Act IV, Scenes 1, 2, and 3

Summary

Scene 1 takes place at the camp of Octavius and his forces, near Alexandria. Octavius (Caesar) receives the letter from Antony, resents that Antony has called him "Boy," and refuses to fight a duel with him. Mecenas wisely suggests that Octavius take full advantage of Antony's angry and irrational behavior and be careful not to become angry himself. Octavius mentions that enough men have defected from Antony's forces to assure Octavius' victory.

In Scene 2 at Cleopatra's palace in Alexandria, Antony learns from Enobarbus that Octavius will not fight a duel with him. He discusses the coming land battle and invites his friends to a lavish dinner. He bids his leaders farewell and alludes to the "last supper" Jesus ate with his disciples, another anachronism. Enobarbus upbraids Antony for the defeatist speech to his comrades, but Antony insists he did not mean it in that manner. Notice Cleopatra's "asides" to Enobarbus, asking what Antony meant by his words.

Scene 3 takes place where some soldiers are keeping watch near Cleopatra's palace. The soldiers hear sounds of revelry, apparently coming from beneath the pavement where they are standing. One soldier says that it is the sound of Hercules, from whom Antony claimed descent, now leaving him. They agree it is an ominous omen for Antony.

Analysis

For a day and a half, Antony begins to resemble the great Mark Antony of his younger years. His contempt for Octavius still oozes from his language, but he can inspire his men and overcome blows, such as the defection of Enobarbus. Now that he has a chance to fight on land, rather than sea, he can out-general Octavius and win the day.

Eros and Enobarbus, two of Antony's closest friends, are contrasted here. Throughout the play to this point, Enobarbus has occupied the superior position and was entrusted with more responsibility than was Eros. But it is Enobarbus who defects to the enemy, and Eros who stays with his friend and commander to the moment of their deaths. The audience may ponder what it was in the characters of the two men that caused the proverbial tables to be turned, nearly at the end of the play, and demonstrated that Eros was, in fact, the superior man, whereas, throughout almost the entire play, Enobarbus was given that position.

Never resolved is why Cleopatra's navy deserted her and Antony. The audience is to assume that Cleopatra did indeed love Antony, probably as much as such a woman could love any man. Could she not control the commanders of her navy? Did she know she could not do so? If she did know, why had she not warned Antony? She had boasted of her naval strength only days before the treachery. In the first sea battle, her ships had fled, with Cleopatra aboard. Could she not have controlled her admirals? She did not protect Antony when presumably she could have done so, nor was she willing to risk herself to descend from her "monument" to kiss and talk with her dying Antony; she insisted that he be raised up to where she was. Perhaps the audience is to understand that a woman such as Cleopatra could not truly love anyone but herself.

At the moment of Antony's death, the conflict of emotions within Cleopatra must have been heavy. She knew that the immediate cause of his death was her arranging to have a false report of her own suicide brought to him. That she should have done such a thing strongly indicates her own immaturity and lack of self-confidence—even a desperate psychological need to find out if Antony really cared about her. She had thought, too late, that her plot might

have caused his suicide; a fully mature woman probably would have thought of that possibility before she initiated the plot. On the other hand, she had had sufficient control of her faculties to realize that once she was in the clutches of Octavius' soldiers, it would be difficult for her to follow Antony in suicide. Therefore, she had made arrangements for the delivery of the figs, with the asps hidden in the bottom of the basket. This planning indicates considerable emotional maturity, suicide was considered an honorable act in Shakespeare's times.

Antony's strong feelings for Cleopatra is not disputed; did he really love her or was it simply "sex appeal"? Antony deserted his men in the first sea battle to chase Cleopatra, who swore later that she was not responsible for the flight of her ships, and Antony believed her. Perhaps she really thought that Antony would not follow her until the battle was over.

In the last analysis, the reader must believe that Antony was not responsible for his final defeat. Shakespeare offers no help in this respect, other than to tacitly suggest that his great fault was to team up with Cleopatra in the first place.

In Scene 1, Antony should have known that Octavius would refuse to fight the duel. If he really did know that, the challenge would have been symbolic, but here, once again, Antony's emotions have overruled his intellect, as Mecenas well knew. It was that knowledge that allowed Mecenas to suggest that Octavius take full advantage of Antony's angry and irrational behavior and be careful not to become angry himself.

In Scene 2, Cleopatra senses that Antony's mind might be cracking under the strain of the previous defeat. Enobarbus' replies offer her precious little encouragement. Enobarbus, perhaps Antony's most trusted friend and soldier, had already planned to defect to Octavius. Therefore, his attitude would be extremely pessimistic about Antony, and he communicates that pessimism to Cleopatra at perhaps the worst time, psychologically, for the queen to hear it.

In Scene 3, there are ghost footsteps. Octavius' soldiers keeping watch there discuss the strange sounds, apparently coming from underneath the pavement. At first they decide it must be the sound of Bacchus departing from the festivities. Were that the case, the omen would have been neutral. But when the soldiers decided it was the sound of Hercules (from whom Antony claimed descent) departing, the omen became obvious: it was extremely unfavorable to Antony and his cause. This entire scene may be taken as foreshadowing Antony's defeat.

Study Questions

1. At the end of Scene 1, Octavius (Caesar) exclaims, "Poor Antony!" Why?

2. Two interchanges of "asides" between Enobarbus and Cleopatra occur close together in Scene 2. About what is Cleopatra worried?

3. What does Antony mean by the line, "Scant not my cups."

4. For what does Enobarbus mildly rebuke his friend and general?

5. How does Antony reply to this rebuke?

6. To what or whom does the term "my hearts" near the end of Scene 2 refer?

7. In Scene 3, what do the soldiers hear that surprises them?

8. Why were the soldiers on guard that night?

9. They attribute what they hear as an evil omen. Why?

10. Who was Hercules and why would an omen concerning him also concern Antony?

Answers

1. Octavius (Caesar) is sure that so many of Antony's men have deserted that victory will be easy.

2. Cleopatra thinks Antony might have given up totally or might be going insane from the defeat.

3. Antony is telling his friends and servants to let the wine (and food) flow freely.

4. Enobarbus upbraids Antony for saying something that made his followers weep.

5. Antony says he did not mean his comments in that way; they were not uttered in "too dolorous a sense" and he actually had intended them for the comfort (strengthening) of his men.

6. The term "my hearts" refers to the same people to which the earlier term "My hearty friends" referred—namely, the soldiers and attendants surrounding Antony.

7. The soldiers hear the sound of music apparently coming from underneath the pavement.

8. The soldiers were guarding against a surprise attack from the enemy.

9. In those days, anything not readily explained by natural causes was interpreted as being some kind of omen from the gods.

10. Antony had claimed descent from the superman/god Hercules, so a sound that would be interpreted as that of Hercules departing from Antony would be considered an evil omen for Antony.

Suggested Essay Topics

1. Many of Antony's men defected to Octavius, but many did not. Why did those who remained loyal to Antony do so, especially after Antony himself gave them permission to defect. Does this fact shed any light on Antony's character? If so, what? What do you think happened to those who remained loyal to Antony after Antony committed suicide?

2. In Scene 2, the mood seems to swing from depressed to jubilant; in Scene 3 it swings back to depressed. How much do you think Mark Antony's comments caused or affected this mood change? Should Antony have made the remarks that might have changed the mood either way? Could he have avoided making them and still have been honest with himself and the others around him? Should those around Antony have been so affected by his remarks? Would you have been, had you been one of Antony's soldiers? Why, or why not?

Act IV, Scenes 4, 5, and 6

Summary

In Scene 4 at Cleopatra's palace in Egypt the next morning, Eros and Cleopatra are helping Antony don his armor as they discuss the prospects of the day. Cleopatra retires to her chamber, and Antony and his men go forth into battle.

Scene 5 takes place on the battlefield just before the battle begins. Antony learns that his close friend Enobarbus has deserted to Octavius. With a show of magnanimity, he sends Enobarbus' trunk and "treasure" to him in Octavius' camp.

At Octavius' camp in Scene 6, Octavius orders his men to take Antony alive. Octavius also has ordered his commanders to put the men who have deserted to him from Antony's forces into the front lines, so that they will be the first to die and Antony will have to kill those who were once his own men. Enobarbus, informed that Antony has sent him his possessions, cannot believe it and tells the messenger he may have them. The messenger assures him that it is true, and Enobarbus is stricken to the core by Antony's love and magnanimity.

Analysis

In Scene 4, Antony's lines are among his finest in the play and represent the old or "real" Antony as he sets out for battle. In Scene 5, Antony's loving gesture in sending Enobarbus his possessions is typical of the old Antony and suggests that he has regained the stature he once had as the commanding general of the triumvirate's forces. It suggests that a good and successful day is about to follow for Antony, as, indeed, it does. The suggestion that Antony took this action to "punish" Enobarbus and to make him "smart" for this treasonous defection has no support in the text of the play or in the meager historical records available to us. That it has an evil effect on Enobarbus and, in fact, does cause him to commit suicide (or, at least, to die) does not prove, or even suggest, that Antony intended it in this manner.

In Scene 6, Octavius' order that his commanders put into the front lines the men who have deserted to him from Antony's forces is, yet, another illustration of the depraved condition of Octavius' mind. Such men will be the first to die, and Antony will have to kill those who were once his own men. Nevertheless, some commanders of high integrity today might have done the same thing, were the battle being fought today. The sight of one's own men in the enemy's front lines might have discouraged the commander from fighting the battle at all and thus might have led to a negotiated instead of a military solution, although this possibility appears strained, at best. Highly significant here is the comment by Octavius' (Caesar) unnamed soldier, who informs Enobarbus of Antony's loving gesture. The soldier says, "Your emperor continues still a Jove," comparing him to Jupiter (Jove), king of the gods in Roman mythology. It is a startling comment from a soldier in the opposing army, and another instance in which Shakespeare uses an unnamed player to utter an important line.

Study Questions

1. Antony was successful in the early fighting described in this act, whereas he had failed miserably in the fighting described in Act III. Why was Antony so successful in Act IV, when he was so unsuccessful in Act III?

2. Antony says to Cleopatra, "Thou art/The armourer of my heart." Why does he mildly and lovingly reprove the queen with that remark?

3. How does Cleopatra feel as she utters the last three lines of Scene 4?

4. What loving act does Antony perform in Scene 5 before the great battle begins?

5. How does Shakespeare's portrayal of this act exhibit his feelings about Antony?

6. Octavius (Caesar), in Scene 6, performs an ugly act, which the playwright depicts immediately following Antony's loving act. What did Octavius do?

7. Does this contrast oppose or reinforce the playwright's implicit comparison of Antony and Octavius?

8. Enobarbus, in a rather tragic soliloquy in Scene 6, tells the audience what happened to Alexas. Here Shakespeare, in a rare, explicit, philosophical comment, addresses the audience and draws an important moral. What is the moral?

9. What is Enobarbus' reaction when one of Octavius' soldiers tells him that Antony has sent to him his "treasure" and his personal belongings?

10. How does the soldier reply to Enobarbus' comment?

Answers

1. Antony was successful early in Act IV because the battle was fought on land, where he had much experience and competence, instead of on the sea (as in Act III), where he had little of either.

2. Cleopatra was trying to help Antony put on his armor for the ensuing battle, but she knows little or nothing about armor and botches the job. He chides her lovingly by saying that her function, performed successfully, is to armor not his body but his heart.

3. Cleopatra is worried and doubts that Antony can win the ensuing battle.

4. Antony sends Enobarbus, who has deserted, his possessions.

5. Shakespeare considers Antony a greater man than Octavius (Caesar); only a great man would perform such a loving act for one who had deserted him.

6. Octavius put the men who had defected to him from Antony's forces in the forefront of the battle, so that Antony and his army would have to kill those who were once their own men.

7. While Shakespeare offers a realistic portrayal of both Antony and Octavius, Antony almost always receives the better treatment. This incident is one of the most obvious examples of the playwright's feelings about the relative merits of the two triumvirs.

8. The almost inevitable result of personal betrayal is disaster to the one who betrays. Here, Alexas is described as betraying his master Antony and persuading Herod the Great instead of Antony. Octavius had Alexas hanged, while Camidius and others who defected from Antony's forces were treated with distrust but were not killed.

9. Enobarbus does not believe him and sarcastically tells the soldier that he may take anything that Antony sent.

10. The soldier assures Enobarbus that what he told him is true,

and that Antony remains a "Jove," that is, a true god. (The Romans considered that Jupiter, or Jove, as he usually was called, was the king of the gods.)

Suggested Essay Topics

1. Did the fact that Cleopatra tried to help Antony don his armor for the coming battle indicate anything about her real feeling about Antony? Were her actions in this respect natural or forced? It became obvious that she knew almost nothing about armor, eliciting from Antony the well-known comment, "Thou art/The armourer of my heart." What does this remark indicate, if anything, about Antony's real feelings about Cleopatra? Would this interchange of remarks be likely to affect Antony's activities during the approaching battle? Why, or why not?

2. In the three-line speech near the beginning of Scene 6, Octavius (Caesar) says, "The time of universal peace is near." What did he mean? The comment could have been immensely significant for Octavius himself and perhaps for all the world. Was this an expression of hope, an augury of the future, or an attempt to build up his own spirit and that of Dolabella in advance of the approaching battle? Why?

Act IV, Scenes 7, 8, and 9

Summary

Scene 7 takes place on the battlefield. Several hours have passed since the last scene, and Octavius' forces are in retreat before the victorious forces of Antony. Scarrus, although wounded, is game for more of the battle. His courage and enthusiasm greatly encourage Antony, who responds as the great military commander he once was and appears to be again now.

Scene 8 occurs a bit later, when the forces loyal to Antony realize that they have won the battle (although not yet the war). Antony sends messengers to Cleopatra to tell her of the victory and ask her to prepare to receive the heroes, particularly Scarrus, as

her guests. Cleopatra appears and embraces Antony in a manner befitting a great and successful military commander. She offers Scarrus a suit of armor made of gold and prepares a victory banquet, even though the war is not yet won.

Scene 9 takes place at the edge of Octavius' camp. Enobarbus, talking to himself, upbraids himself for his cowardly act in deserting Antony, then dies. The guards hear the monologue, listening for something that might be of use to their commander, Octavius. Then they carry off Enobarbus' body.

Analysis

In Scene 7, Scarrus' courage and desire to continue fighting, although wounded, greatly encourage Antony, who responds as the great military commander he once was and appears to be again now. This is another example of Shakespeare's understanding of human psychology. Here the commanding general draws strength and courage from the courage and enthusiasm of one with a rank well beneath his own. Any experienced and high-ranking military or naval officer can tell stories of how exactly the same thing has happened to him/her—how he/she has been strengthened and encouraged by the enthusiasm and courage of just one underling.

In Scene 8, notice the pun on guests/gests (line 2), the latter word meaning, in Elizabethan times, deeds of valor. In Scene 9, a sentry is probably a lower-echelon officer, something like a centurion. The guard he commands is there to give warning if Antony should launch a surprise attack. Enobarbus' dying speech suggests that he was dying from self-inflicted wounds, probably both internal and external. Nevertheless, it was a common supposition in Shakespeare's day (and earlier) that one might actually die of a broken heart, given the proper circumstances, without any other cause of death.

Study Questions

1. What is the meaning of Agrippa's comment at the opening of Scene 7?

2. How does Scarrus react to the existing situation?

3. What does Scarrus mean by saying, "I'll halt after"?

4. What did Antony mean by referring to "Hectors" at the beginning of Scene 8?

5. What does Cleopatra promise Scarrus for his bravery and valiant behavior?

6. In Scene 9, what is Enobarbus' attitude?

7. Why did Enobarbus die?

8. Octavius' soldiers overhear Enobarbus' soliloquy just before his death. What is their reaction to what he is saying?

9. What does the sentry mean by saying, "He is of note"?

10. What was the soldiers' attitude toward Enobarbus?

Answers

1. Agrippa realizes that the forces of Octavius (Caesar) have suffered a decisive defeat, and he orders a retreat. He realizes Octavius and his army are in a bad spot and have a great deal to do to recover from the defeat.

2. Although seriously wounded, Scarrus is jubilant and is willing to receive far more wounds the next day in completing Antony's victory.

3. Scarrus realizes that he cannot keep up with Antony and the others as they go toward Cleopatra's palace, but he says that he will limp along.

4. Hector, son of Priam, king of Troy fought valiantly for Troy until he was defeated by the Greek warrior Achilles in the famous battle. Therefore, a valiant warrior was often referred to as a "Hector."

5. Cleopatra promises Scarrus a suit of golden armor.

6. Enobarbus repents deeply of his actions as a traitor to his beloved Antony and calls upon the moon to be a witness to his repentance. He probably is aware he is about to die.

7. Shakespeare does not tell us whether Enobarbus died at his own hand or died of a broken heart—broken by his own cowardice in defecting to Octavius (Caesar).

8. The soldiers think that what Enobarbus is saying might affect (or be of interest to) their commander, Octavius.

9. The sentry means that Enobarbus is (or was) an important officer in Octavius' army.

10. The soldiers' attitude is one of relative sympathy and even understanding, in spite of the fact that Enobarbus was a member of the opposing army. They try to minister to him as best they are able, but Enobarbus is already dead.

Suggested Essay Topics

1. Why did Enobarbus defect to Octavius' forces, and how did that defection lead to his death soon thereafter? Do you think he died of a broken heart, or did he actually commit suicide (by taking poison, for instance)? How much effect, if any, did his defection have on Antony?

2. Scarrus' bravery and courage greatly strengthen Antony, as they talk after Antony's big victory in the land action against Octavius (Caesar). Antony intends to see that Scarrus is properly rewarded by Cleopatra, as indeed he is. But then, following this battle, Enobarbus deeply repents (Scene 9) of his defection from Antony and then dies. Does Antony gain as much, psychologically, from Scarrus' bravery and courage as he lost from Enobarbus' defection? Does Antony's great victory in battle that day explain the sorrow and humiliation Enobarbus feels just before he dies? Did Enobarbus' defection have anything to do with Scarrus' magnificent performance that day? Why, or why not?

Act IV, Scenes 10, 11, and 12

Summary

Scene 10 takes place near Antony's headquarters, the following morning. Antony is surveying the situation to determine how to handle the second day of the battle. He notes that Octavius is preparing for a sea battle. Antony is fighting his battle on earth and water and wishes he also could fight Octavius in air and in fire. Scene 11 has only four lines as Octavius (Caesar) views the situation from a point near his camp. Octavius tells his troops his best advantage, after yesterday's defeat, is to attack by sea.

In Scene 12 at a vantage point overlooking the sea where the battle is to be joined, Antony and Scarrus see Cleopatra's ships desert and go to Octavius' side. Antony knows that their treachery ends his chance for a victory. He blames Cleopatra for ordering the treachery and calls her a whore. He orders Scarrus to tell his forces to give up the battle, then he launches into a bitter tirade against Cleopatra. When she appears, he tells her to leave immediately, or he'll kill her. She leaves.

Analysis

In Scene 10, a foreshadowing of disaster for Antony is revealed in an expression of his overconfidence. In his day, people believed there were only four elements: earth, air, fire, and water. Antony, fighting his battle on earth and water, wishes he also could fight Octavius in air and in fire. This statement has been taken as Shakespeare's prophecy that battles of the future would be fought in the air and with fire, but the possibility appears, at best, strained and, at worst, ludicrous. In Shakespearean drama, a display of undue pride often foretells a fall.

Scene 11 is another short transition scene that allows the audience to see the picture from Octavius' standpoint.

In Scene 12, Shakespeare offers no real evidence that Cleopatra had anything to do with the desertion of her sailors and ships. Insofar as the audience can determine, the playwright assigns the cause to pure cowardice on the part of Cleopatra's sailors (and, perhaps, the poor state of repair of their boats, which had been mentioned earlier in the play). Antony thinks she intended to become Octavius' woman—another wrong guess on Antony's part. The "shirt of Nessus" is a shirt Hercules' wife, Deianira, had given him, smeared with the blood of the centaur Nessus whom Hercule—also sometimes called Alcides—had shot with a poisoned arrow. Deianira had thought the blood on the shirt would work as a love charm, but instead it caused Hercules such great and searing pain that he flung the servant who had brought the shirt to him so high in the air that he fell into the sea far from land and died. This is yet another reference to Hercules, from whom Antony claimed descent.

Study Questions

1. The later fighting in Act IV was disastrous to Antony for two highly important reasons. What were they?

2. In Scene 10, what does Antony mean when he says, "I would they'd fight i'th'fire or i'th'air"?

3. At the beginning of Scene 12, Scarrus says, "Swallows have built/In Cleopatra's sails their nests." What does he mean?

4. What is the meaning of Scarrus' comment about the "augurers"?

5. Antony, seeing Cleopatra's ships once again give up the fight, but this time defect to Octavius (Caesar), calls Cleopatra a "Triple-turned whore." To what is he referring?

6. Antony tells Scarrus to "Bid them all fly." What is Scarrus being instructed to do?

7. What does Antony threaten to do to Cleopatra?

8. Antony's reference to his wife Octavia in line 38 of Scene 12 implies a comparison between Octavia and Cleopatra. How does Antony compare the two women?

9. Who is the "young Roman boy" Antony mentions in his soliloquy at the end of Scene 12?

10. What is Antony's general attitude during Scene 12?

Answers

1. Antony knew little about sea battles, and Cleopatra's fleet, on which he had counted heavily, defected to Octavius' side.

2. In ancient Rome, educated people believed that everything was composed of some mixture of only four elements: earth, air, fire, and water. Antony had fought and defeated Octavius (Caesar) on the earth and was about to fight him on the sea; exulting in the previous day's victory, Antony says that, hav-

ing fought Octavius on the earth and on the sea, he'd like to fight him also in the fire and in the air.

3. Scarrus is speaking symbolically; it is hardly likely that swallows would build nests in sails. "Sails" here is used as a synecdoche, as it is elsewhere in this and other plays. Scarrus says that the swallows have built nests in Cleopatra's ships; that is an evil omen in the minds of ancient Romans and probably Egyptians, too. Furthermore, if her ships are sufficiently idle to allow birds to build nests in them, one might conclude that her sailors are not properly trained and ready to do battle.

4. In essence, Scarrus says the Soothsayers know that Antony's forces are to be destroyed by Octavius (Caesar), but that they are afraid to say so—and probably justifiably afraid. Antony has not been lenient with those who bring bad news, nor has Cleopatra.

5. Cleopatra was the lover of Julius Caesar (to whom she bore Caesarion), then of Pompey, and then of Antony. She was false to them and betrayed all of her lovers.

6. Antony is instructing Scarrus to tell the soldiers to leave him and go to Octavius.

7. Antony threatens to kill Cleopatra.

8. Octavia comes out of the comparison as a much better person than Cleopatra. An angry Antony overreacts, of course, and suggests that his patient wife Octavia should be permitted to "plough" Cleopatra's face with her fingernails. This constitutes about as grim a statement as a man could make about his erstwhile lover.

9. The "young Roman boy" is Octavius (Caesar), to whom Antony usually refers to as a "mere lad."

10. Antony is thoroughly disgusted and discouraged with himself and with Cleopatra; he is considering killing her and then committing suicide.

Suggested Essay Topics

1. Antony so exults in his victory over Octavius (Caesar) that he says he wishes he could fight Octavius in the fire and the air as well as on the land and the sea. Is he overconfident at this point? Does this comment indicate hatred of Octavius? Disgust with him? Or simply annoyance with him? Had it been within Antony's power to simply disintegrate Octavius and all his army by waving a magic wand, would Antony have done that? Or would he have refused such an opportunity

and chosen to attempt to defeat his enemy in a prosaic land and/or sea battle? Why?

2. In Scene 12, Antony blames Cleopatra and her ships for his defeat and calls her a "triple-turned whore." Was either charge against Cleopatra justified, or was Antony simply overreacting to the situation, as he often did? No excuse whatever is offered anywhere in the play for the cowardly acts of the Egyptian ships, nor does the queen herself defend that action. Unlike in the action at Actium, she was not aboard any of the ships when they and their crews defected to Octavius. Do you think that Antony's flight at Actium in search of Cleopatra had anything to do with the defection of the queen's navy at the battle of Alexandria? Why, or why not?

Act IV, Scenes 13 and 14

New Characters:

Diomedes: *attendent of Cleopatra*

Decretas (Dercetus): *friend of Mark Antony*

Summary

Scene 13 takes place in Cleopatra's palace. Cleopatra tells Charmian that Antony has gone insane. Indeed, this is a reasonable conclusion, considering the emotional manner in which Antony has been speaking. Then, at Charmian's suggestion, she tells Mardian to tell Antony that she is dead and to report back to her, at her monument (which was built as her tomb), how Antony takes this news.

Scene 14 takes place on a promontory near Cleopatra's palace, overlooking the battlefields and probably also the harbor where the sea battle took place. Antony discusses with Eros the tragedy of his defeat. Mardian arrives with (false) news that Cleopatra died with Antony's name on her lips. Antony, in a bit of bitter comic relief, has been comparing himself to a shadow on the water. Antony now asks Eros to fulfill an old promise to kill him, assuring him that by killing Antony, it is Octavius (Caesar) that he

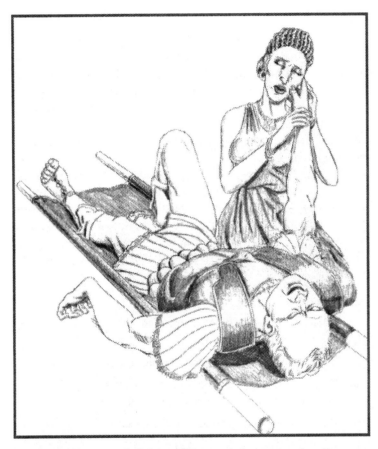

will defeat. But Eros kills himself instead. Antony praises Eros as a worthier man than himself, then tries to commit suicide by falling on his own sword, but botches the job. Decretas sees Antony in his near-dead condition with his bloody sword nearby. He realizes that if he carries this sword to Octavius (Caesar) he will earn himself forever a seat in Octavius' court, so he does so.

Antony begs the guards to come and kill him, but they refuse. Then Diomedes comes to him from Cleopatra. Antony asks Diomedes to kill him, but Diomedes says that Cleopatra is alive and was afraid that Antony might harm himself, thinking she was dead. Antony asks his guards to carry him to where Cleopatra is and assures them it will be the last service he asks of them.

Analysis

In Scene 13, having Mardian tell Antony that Cleopatra has committed suicide is her immature way to get back at Antony for his blistering condemnation of her when he thought she was responsible for the defection of the Egyptian ships. A more psychologically mature woman would have realized instantly the possible disastrous consequences of such a plot. Of course, Cleopatra did realize the consequences later, but too late to prevent Antony from trying to kill himself.

In Scene 14, notice the string of similes in the opening lines: "a cloud that's dragonish." etc. Eros, long before, had been Antony's bondservant. When Antony had freed him, he had sworn to Antony that, should Antony ever ask him to do so, he would kill Antony. Notice the double entendre in line 105: "I have done my work ill, friends." can apply both to Antony's botched attempt at suicide and his handling of the entire war with Octavius.

Study Questions

1. What advice does Charmian give Cleopatra after Antony has threatened to kill the queen?

2. What is Cleopatra's reaction to Antony's threat?

3. Why does Cleopatra retire to her monument (tomb)? What does this action indicate about her character?

4. Who brings the news of Cleopatra's "death" to Antony?

5. What is Antony's reply to the emissary?

6. What is the essence of Antony's soliloquy after Eros has left the stage temporarily?

7. Why does Mark Antony decide to die at that particular time?

8. How does Eros avoid the bitterly unpleasant task of killing his beloved Mark Antony when he had promised years before to do so if Antony asked him?

9. What is Antony's reaction to what Eros did?

10. What does Decretas do after Antony attempts suicide?

Answers

1. Charmian suggests that Cleopatra flee to her monument (which contains her tomb) and send a message to Antony that she has committed suicide.

2. Cleopatra thinks that Antony has gone insane.

3. Cleopatra retires to her monument for safety; Antony had threatened to kill her because her navy had defected to Octavius. Here her fear is to some extent realistic, but her attempt to learn how Antony would react to her "death" is, at best, immature. She should have known, before she sent Mardian to him, that her scheme might cause Antony to commit suicide.

4. Mardian bears the (false) sad news to Antony.

5. Antony tells Mardian that his reward is that he is allowed to leave Antony's presence without being killed.

6. Antony addresses the queen, whom he believes to be dead, and promises to join her quickly in death, after which they will roam together through the hereafter.

7. Antony decides to die then because he knows he has lost the war, and he has been informed that Cleopatra is dead.

8. Eros kills himself instead of Mark Antony.

9. Antony says that Eros is "thrice nobler" than himself; then he himself tries to commit suicide by falling on his sword, but succeeds only in wounding himself.

10. Decretas steals Antony's bloody sword and plans to take it to Octavius (Caesar) and use it to obtain mercy and high standing for himself.

Suggested Essay Topics

1. To what extent can Cleopatra be blamed for Antony's suicide? Was the fault hers or Antony's, or was it simply a matter of fate, in which neither person can be blamed? How does Cleopatra's character, as portrayed in the play to this point, explain why she acted as she did?

2. At the beginning of Scene 14, Antony says to Eros (probably the one major character still intensely loyal to him), "Sometimes we see a cloud that's dragonish." Is Antony, at this point, totally insane, gradually going insane, or merely trying to relax after a humiliating defeat (for which he blamed Cleopatra and her ships and sailors)? From Eros' replies to Antony, how do you think Eros himself viewed the situation?

3. In your opinion, does Shakespeare drag out the matter of the death of Antony too long, when the same effect could have been produced with fewer lines, or is each line absolutely necessary to achieve the effect Shakespeare desired? Mention which lines might have been omitted with little or no loss of effect, if you find any that fit that description.

Act IV, Scene 15

Summary

This scene takes place in Alexandria, at Cleopatra's monument, which contains the tomb she has built for herself. Antony has been brought to the monument. He begs Cleopatra to come down and kiss him before he dies, but she refuses, saying it's too dangerous. But she and her attendants manage to hoist Antony up to where Cleopatra is. Antony and Cleopatra exchange a few lines before he dies. In his typical spirit of magnanimity, Antony tells Cleopatra to seek both her honor and her safety with Octavius. She protests that, here, honor and safety are incompatible. Cleopatra vows to give Antony a real Roman funeral.

Analysis

In Scene 15, Cleopatra protests, after Antony has told her to seek honor and safety with Octavius (Caesar), that, here, honor and safety are incompatible—a line that shows her in a favorable light, especially to an audience of Shakespeare's day. She has matured considerably, probably as a result of the crisis of the recent days, and determines to kill herself. In Elizabethan times, suicide was considered an honorable act; thus, Cleopatra, in making and carrying out this determination, exhibits a maturity that has been severely lacking in her character up to this point.

Study Questions

1. Why does Cleopatra refuse to come down from her monument to kiss the dying Antony one last time? Is this an indication of her character or of her true feelings about Antony?

2. What does Cleopatra do instead of emerging from her monument?

3. Cleopatra says, "If knife, drugs, serpents, have/Edge, sting, or operation, I am safe." What does she mean?

4. Cleopatra says, a few lines later, "Had I great Juno's power,/ The strong-winged Mercury should fetch thee up/And set thee by Jove's side." About whom is she talking?

5. Whom does Antony, before he dies, tell the queen to trust?

6. What advice does he give the queen at that time?

7. Why does Iras say, "She's dead too, our sovereign"?

8. At the end of the act, Cleopatra asks, "Then is it sin/To rush into the secret house of death/Ere death dare come to us?" About what is the queen speaking?

9. What does Cleopatra's question indicate about Egyptian philosophy prevalent in Cleopatra's time?

10. What does Cleopatra promise the dead Antony?

Answers

1. Cleopatra refuses to leave the monument because she is afraid she'll be killed or taken prisoner if she leaves that place of relative safety. In this instance, her head probably is ruling her heart. Cleopatra's extensive physical effort (and that of her two attendants) to raise Antony to the upper level substantially mitigates her failure to rush to him and dramatizes her real love for him.

2. Cleopatra and her attendants manage to lift the dying Antony up into the monument, so that she can kiss him and exchange a few lines with him before he dies.

3. Cleopatra refers to the means she has available for committing suicide and asserts that as long as she has these means available to her, she can kill herself anytime she wants to do so.

4. Juno, wife of the chief god Jove (Jupiter), had the power to command Mercury to lift Antony's dying body to the balcony of the monument where Cleopatra and her attendants would be waiting. (As it is, the women must perform that task themselves.)

5. Antony tells the queen to trust, of all Octavius' men, only Proculeius.

6. Antony tells her to seek her honor and her safety with Octavius (Caesar).

7. Cleopatra has fainted—in this case a real and not a feigned faint—and Iras thinks she is dead.

8. The queen is speaking about suicide and asking (rhetorically) if suicide was a sin.

9. The fact that she should ask if suicide was a sin indicates that the existing Egyptian culture might have considered suicide, at least under certain circumstances, sinful.

10. Cleopatra promises the dead Antony a funeral in "the high Roman fashion."

Suggested Essay Topics

1. Cleopatra refused to descend from her monument to tend to the dying Antony, for fear that she might be "taken." What does this refusal say about her real feelings about him? A few lines earlier she had said to Charmian, her chief attendant and confidante, that she would "never go from hence." If she thought she would never leave her monument under any conditions anyway, why was she afraid to go the side of her dying lover? Is she more interested in avoiding capture by

the forces of Octavius (Caesar) than she is in comforting Antony? If so, is that not an indication of intense selfishness on her part? Would you have followed Cleopatra's example and remained in the monument, or would you have cast caution to the wind and rushed to the dying lover's side? Why, or why not?

2. What is Cleopatra's mood after Antony dies and she is alone with Charmian and Iras? Her speech at the end of Scene 15 is one of the most tragic in all of Shakespeare's works. Is she getting exactly what she deserves, or is she the victim of circumstances totally beyond her control? Why?

SECTION SIX

Act V

Act V, Scenes 1 and 2

New Characters:

Proculeius: *friend of Mark Antony*

Seleucus: *attendant to Cleopatra (and her treasurer)*

Clown: *brings the deadly asps to Cleopatra*

Summary

Scene 1 takes place in Octavius' camp outside Alexandria. Octavius (Caesar) learns from Decretas that Antony is dead, the message verified by Decretas' presentation to Octavius of Antony's sword, stained with the triumvir's own blood. Octavius weeps for him, uttering another of the famous Shakespearan passages: "The Breaking of so great a thing should make/a greater Crack." He says that the world should shake to its very foundations and everything in it be upset by the death of so great a man as Antony. Afterwards Agrippa says, in another well-known passage, "But you Gods will give us/Some Faults to make us Men." Octavius muses that it might have been Antony who became sole ruler of the world instead of himself.

A messenger from Cleopatra arrives to ask Octavius how she should prepare for whatever he should order her to do. He offers a peaceful answer, but then sends Proculeius (and Gallus, who does not speak in most extant manuscripts of this play) to Cleopatra

with kind words, fearing that she, like Antony, might commit suicide. But Octavius is crafty and intends to physically seize the queen while her attention is distracted by talking with Octavius' emissary, Proculeius (and, presumably, Gallus).

Scene 2 takes place in Cleopatra's monument. Cleopatra, Charmian, Iras, and Mardian are there when Proculeius enters. He tells the queen that she will be treated well by the emperor, but while he is saying so, soldiers enter to seize her. They take from her a dagger with which she had intended to commit suicide. Nevertheless, she threatens suicide or, at the very least, disfigurement, and Proculeius tries desperately to dissuade her, knowing that her suicide will foil the emperor's plans for her (and, incidentally, subject Proculeius to possible disciplinary action by Octavius). Dolabella enters and tells Proculeius that Octavius has sent for him and that he may leave, that he (Dolabella) will assume responsibility for the queen's safety and that of her retinue.

Cleopatra tells Dolabella about a dream she has had about a magnificent Antony who seems far beyond other men in stature and magnificence. She asks Dolabella if such a man could exist. He replies in the negative, but feels great sympathy for Cleopatra and tells her, albeit reluctantly, that Octavius intends to parade her through the streets of Rome as a prize of war.

Octavius (Caesar) enters, speaks kind words to Cleopatra, and she replies, pretending abject submission to him. But Octavius warns her against committing suicide and tells her that, should she do so, things will go hard with her children. She offers him what she says is her entire treasure, but her treasurer Seleucus denies that fact and says it is only about half her treasure. Furious at this treason from one of her attendants, she blushes, but Octavius congratulates her on her foresight in holding something back. She says part of what was held back was intended as a present for Livia (Octavius' wife) and Octavia. She asks Octavius to leave, which he does, along with his retinue.

In a bitter conversation with Iras and Charmian, the queen tells them how they will be treated if Octavius takes them to Rome. Iras replies that she's sure that her nails are stronger than her eyes—that is, that she will tear out her eyes before she will submit to such humiliation.

Cleopatra, with considerable foresight, already has provided a relatively painless way for her, and possibly for her attendants, to kill themselves. A "rural man" (later identified as the Clown) arrives with what purportedly is a basket of figs, but actually contains several asps hidden beneath the figs. Cleopatra questions him about the asps and asks if he personally knows of anyone actually killed by them. He replies that he knows many. Here Shakespeare introduces a long period of comic relief , during which Cleopatra tries to get rid of the Clown, who obviously does not want to leave but rather to enjoy his hour in the sun with the queen and her court.

Eventually the Clown does leave, but just before he would have been bodily thrown out of the monument.

Charmian and Iras bring the queen, at her command, the best robe, jewels, and crown. She dons them, stating that it is fitting that she, a royal queen, be dressed in her finest clothes to meet Antony, presumably in the hereafter, for all know that Antony is dead. She bids Iras and Charmian a long farewell, unaware that they too will be dead within seconds. Iras dies first, apparently bit-

ten by one of the asps. Then the queen holds one to her breast,
refers to it as her baby, sucking her to sleep, and dies. Charmian
then grasps an asp, begging it to kill her, which it does.

Dolabella returns to the monument and finds the three women
dead. Then Octavius arrives and is surprised at their deaths, for
there was no blood. But Dolabella finds the "vent of Blood" on
Cleopatra's breast and arm. A soldier finds a trail of slime on the
fig leaves, such as asps leave on the caves of the Nile River, thus
answering for Octavius the question of how the three women died.
Octavius pays them homage, orders that Cleopatra be buried with
"her Antony," and makes plans to give them a huge state funeral,
which all his army shall attend.

Analysis

In Scene 1, Octavius' speech, "O Antony,/I have followed thee
to this," suggests Octavius' psychological maturity, as do the lines
in which he praises his dead opponent as a great man.

In Scene 2, Dolabella apparently outranks Proculeius; otherwise Proculeius would have been reluctant to surrender control of
Cleopatra. In Cleopatra's description of her dream, notice the figures of speech: simile (he was as rattling thunder, dolphin-like,
islands were as plates), synecdoche (crowns and crownets), metaphor (winter, autumn), etc.

Dolabella feels great sympathy for Cleopatra and tells her, albeit reluctantly, that Octavius intends to parade her through the
streets of Rome as a prize of war. In doing so, Dolabella risks his own
life, should Octavius learn of the matter. It gives Dolabella, in the
eyes of the audience, much greater stature than any other servant
of Octavius and, indeed, stature above most other men in the play.

Later in this scene, Cleopatra's remark to the emperor, "Wert
thou a Man,/Thou would'st have Mercy on me," suggests that she
is addressing Octavius, no doubt facetiously, as a god rather than
as a man. The other possibility is that she addresses the remark to
Seleucus, in which case it is an insulting and deprecating remark.

Octavius warns Cleopatra against committing suicide and tells
her that, should she do so, things will go hard with her children.
The viewer of Shakespeare's day probably would have interpreted
that warning as a statement that Octavius will kill all her offspring

if she commits suicide. As mentioned earlier, he did kill one son—Caesarion—whom she had borne by Julius Caesar years before her relationship with Antony began. Octavius thus eliminated another possible claimant to the throne.

Cleopatra, with considerable foresight, already has provided a relatively painless way for her, and possibly for her attendants, to kill themselves. During the long period of comic relief while the Clown is on stage, there is an added point of comic relief produced by the pun on the word "lie" which could mean either to tell a falsehood or to have intercourse with.

As Cleopatra dons her best clothes, intending to meet Antony in the hereafter, it should be remembered that Antony in the previous act, metaphorically called himself a "bridegroom."

Study Questions

1. What, if any, was the international significance of Antony's death?

2. Why was Octavius (Caesar) anxious to prevent Cleopatra's death?

3. What did Dolabella do for Cleopatra that no other of Octavius' officers or soldiers did for her?

4. What was Octavius' approach to Cleopatra after he learned that Antony was dead? Does this approach shed any light on his character, which Shakespeare developed throughout the play? If so, what?

5. What was Cleopatra's reaction to Octavius and his emissaries?

6. Did Octavius intend to kill Cleopatra later?

7. What was the threat Procleius made to Cleopatra to disuade her from committing suicide?

8. Why did Octavius, upon learning of Cleopatra's death, order a huge funeral for her and Antony?

9. Did Octavius make any move to physically harm Cleopatra or her attendants after he learned of Antony's death?

10. What did Octavius intend to do after the funeral for Antony and Cleopatra?

Answers

1. Octavius (Caesar) was then the sole ruler of the civilized world surrounding the Mediterranean Sea. He became known as Caesar Augustus.

2. Octavius wanted to prevent Cleopatra's death because he intended to take her to Rome and parade her as a prize of war.

3. Dolabella warned Cleopatra that Octavius intended to take her to Rome as a prize of war and parade her through the streets as a symbol of his victory.

4. After learning of Antony's death, Octavius was afraid that Cleopatra would commit suicide, so he promised her "half the

world" to dissuade her from her intentions. He said that she could command him as to what her fate should be, but the play suggests that he had no intention of keeping his promises.

5. Even without Dolabella's warning of what Octavius intended, she did not trust him. She pretended to be his vassal, ready to do his will.

6. There is no historical evidence nor evidence within the play that Octavius ever intended to kill Cleopatra. We are not told what he intended to do with her after he displayed her in Rome.

7. Procleius warned Cleopatra that the children would be treated well if she served Octavius' will. This is a veiled threat that he would kill her children if she committed suicide.

8. Octavius wanted to be known as a gentle monarch. As the sole ruler of the world, he could afford to be so.

9. Neither Octavius nor his soldiers attempted to harm Cleopatra—only to restrain her and her attendants from suicide and prevent their escape.

10. Octavius intended to return to Rome with his army after the funeral.

Suggested Essay Topics

1. Did Cleopatra have any reasonable alternatives to suicide? Did Iras and Charmian? To what extent, if any, did her love for Antony contribute to her reason to commit suicide? Had Cleopatra been more mature in her decisions throughout the play, would the play have had a different ending? If so, what are some possible endings?

2. Octavius (Caesar) said that, as supreme emperor, he dare not be other than merciful and gentle. Was he serious and did he really mean so, or were these simply words with no intent behind them? How would you have felt at that point if you had been Octavius? What outward indications in actual actions, if any, demonstrated his real intentions in this respect?

3. In your opinion, did the climax of the play occur when
   Antony committed suicide, when Cleopatra committed suicide, when you learned that Antony would fall before
   Octavius and that Octavius would become sole emperor of
   the world, or at some other point in the play? Why?

Sample Analytical Paper Topics

Topic #1

Antony and Cleopatra was received without enthusiasm by audiences of the early seventeenth century in England. The play has continued to attract attention throughout its nearly 400–year history. Many factors contributed to the audience's reaction to the play. Discuss these issues in your paper.

Outline

I.   Thesis Statement: *Many social factors contributed to the audience's negative reaction to* Antony and Cleopatra *when it was first produced.*

II.   The difference in time (1600 years) and in location (2000 miles) between where the action of the play takes place and where the play was first produced.

   A.   Cultural Differences

      1.   Roman and Egyptian History

      2.   British Drama

   B.   Shakespeare's development of the character Cleopatra, compared to the other characters in the play.

      1.   Influence of the playwright's gender on the development of female and male characters.

III. Factors affecting how *Antony and Cleopatra* was received when it was first produced in England.

   A. By the critics

   B. By the literate public (who expressed their opinions in writing).

   C. By the illiterate public who saw the play performed and expressed their opinions.

IV. Politics that might have affected the way in which *Antony and Cleopatra* was received in England of the early seventeenth century.

   A. The recent union of Scotland and England to become Great Britain.

      1. The political repercussions of the imprisonment in England of Mary Queen of Scots.

   B. Publication of the "King James" English translation of the Bible.

   C. The religious unrest seething in England during the latter part of Shakespeare's lifetime.

      1. The Protestant/Catholic controversies.

      2. The repression of religious freedom of speech and actions.

Topic #2

Shakespeare tends to favor Antony over Octavius (Caesar) as being the better of the two men, even though he honestly portrays the faults of both and the good points of both. Dissect the play to find specific lines or speeches that relate to this distinction, and indicate how they suggest the relative merits of the two leading men. Do you think the playwright preferred Antony? Was his preference based on historical fact or was it merely personal prejudice unrelated to the facts of history?

Outline

I. Thesis Statement: *Shakespeare favored the character of Antony over that of Octavius.*

II. Portrait of Antony

    A. Antony in Egypt at the opening of the play.

    B. Antony in Egypt after the battle of Actium.

    C. Antony before, during, and after the successful land battle against Octavius.

    D. Antony after the sea battle in which Cleopatra's ships joined Octavius.

    E. Antony with Eros just before his attempt at suicide.

III. A portrait of Octavius (Caesar).

    A. Octavius upbraiding Antony upon Antony's return to Rome from Egypt.

    B. Octavius' conference with Mecenas and Agrippa in Rome, detailing Antony's faults.

    C. Octavius receiving news of Antony's death.

    D. Octavius with Cleopatra near the end of the play.

IV. Comparison of the two characterizations.

    A. Depth of characterization.

    B. Accuracy and honesty of characterization.

    C. Personal biases (if any) reflected in the characterizations.

    D. Conclusions about Shakespeare's treatment of these two men in this play.

Topic #3

Locate a modern stage production of *Antony and Cleopatra.* From the newspapers of the city where it was produced notice the reviews and any comments the papers' drama critics might have made about it. Then consider how and why the text of the modern production might have been changed from the original text, what effect the changes had on the modern audiences, and whether the play was considered successful by the drama critics.

Outline

I. Thesis Statement: *It would be difficult to stage Antony and Cleopatra as it was originally produced.*

II. The original text.

    A. Number of acts and scenes.

        1. Scenery used (remembering that no scenery was used in Shakespeare's day)

        2. Should the play be shortened? (The original is one of the longest of all Shakespeare's plays.)

III . Costuming.

    A. Elaborate or simple.

IV. The critics' reactions to the original version.

    A. To the text of the play.

    B. To the quality of the production.

    C. To the financial success of the project.

V. Comments of the theatergoers and reviewers from various newspapers.

Bibliography

Andrews, John F., ed. *William Shakespeare: Antony and Cleopatra.* London, J. M. Dent, 1993.

Baldwin, T. W. *Shakespeare's Five–Act Structure.* Urbana (IL), University of Illinois Press, 1963.

Bevington, David, ed. *William Shakespeare: Antony and Cleopatra.* Cambridge (England), Cambridge University Press, 1990.

Charney, Maurice. *How to Read Shakespeare.* New York, McGraw-Hill, 1971.

—— *Shakespeare's Roman Plays.* Cambridge (MA), Harvard University Press, 1963.

Clough, Arthur Hugh, ed. *Plutarch: The Lives of the Noble Grecians and Romans.* tr. John Dryden. New York, Modern Library [Random House], [1932] (Reprint of eighteenth–century edition.)

Evans, G. Blakemore. *The Riverside Shakespeare.* Boston, Houghton Mifflin, 1974.

Everett, Barbara, ed. *The Tragedy of Antony and Cleopatra.* New York, New American Library [The Signet Classic Shakespeare], 1963.

Haliday, F. E. *A Shakespeare Companion, 1564–1964.* New York, Schocken Books, 1964.

Nicoll, Allardyce, ed. *Shakespeare Survey, Vol. 10.* Cambridge (England), [Cambridge] University Press, 1957.

Ogburn, Dorothy and Charleton. *This Star of England.* Westport (CT), Greenwood Press, 1972 (Reprint of earlier edition. New York, Coward-McCann, 1952).

Ridley, M. R., ed. *Antony and Cleopatra.* London and New York, Methuen, 1965.